The joy of the Lord
is your strength.
Jesus loves you ♡

Nancy Johnson

Ask
FOR YOUR
Miracle

Victory Steps to Receive Healing

ASK FOR YOUR Miracle

Victory Steps to Receive Healing

NANCY ANN JOHNSON

First Edition
Copyright © 2019 Nancy Ann Johnson
First Printing, June 2019

ISBN 9781098769239

Edited by Dave Arns
Formatted by Dave Arns
Cover art by Lynnette Bonner at Indie Cover Design

Contents

Dedication

I dedicate this book to my incredibly loyal and loving husband Richard Johnson and my two champion sons, Christopher and Jeffrey Johnson. These incredible men in my life stood with me through it all. And of course, my wonderful Jesus, thank you that I am alive today.

Endorsements

Ask For Your Miracle is a beautiful book full of warm counsel and great faith in a wonder-working, supernatural God, that will jump-start the release of a new level of heavenly power in your life. Your miracle is waiting for you now! Reach out to God today and receive your miracle.

Joan Hunter
Evangelist/Author
Miracles Happen TV host
Miracles Happen!

Nancy is a wildly passionate woman of God. I have personally watched her story continue to develop over the last almost 10 years.

I witnessed Nancy's tenacious faith grab hold of the healing promise of God, and raise her up from near death. I saw her hunger in many moments in the presence of God. I have experienced her leadership, looking for every opportunity to bring healing and salvation to the lost!

Nancy is the real deal, she loves with a Jesus-style love, and her boldness and risk-taking won't deny her in any situation of touching someone's life! Don't let Nancy's innocence fool you, she is loaded for bear!

Pastor Keith Kippen
Lead Pastor @ Jake's House Church

Nancy Ann Johnson has experienced first-hand the healing power of God after a long season of pain and life-threatening illness. She comes to the table with both personal experience and God-given revelation into the miraculous nature of God. *Ask for Your Miracle* is a must-read book full of key foundational truths and testimonies of God's love and promises fulfilled. This book will take you through a step-by-step guide in building your faith and relationship with the Lord as it impacts and encourages your spirit.

Daniel Kolenda
President and C.E.O.
Christ for all Nations

In reading Nancy's book you can see she is absolutely in love with Jesus. Her love for Jesus shines through in every page.

Nancy is a deeply spiritual woman with so much to impart to her readers. Her walk matches her talk. I have known Nancy now for many years. Her hunger for more revelation of the work of God has been her secret in her healing.

The Holy Spirit will use this book to minister to your heart. Nancy is a fully devoted follower of Jesus. She never gave up when times were tough. It is my honor to recommend this book.

Fran L. Lance
Free Lance MINISTRIES

Introduction

"Mr. Johnson, does your wife have a Living Will? We need you to bring us a copy of her file. We need to know her wishes in case we are forced to make some hard decisions."

This question was posed to me three or four times by doctors and the nursing staff during one week in February of 2009. I answered, "Yes, she does," but I refused to bring it to the hospital. In my mind, that was not going to happen and was not a consideration. I was drawing on faith that I really didn't know if I had.

It had come to this. We were in critical care at Skagit Valley Hospital. Tests showed that my wife Nancy was depleted of necessary minerals and her core body temperature had dropped to 85 degrees. This was the result of years of perceived food allergies and chemical sensitivities. Then if we didn't get her stabilized, she was at risk of her internal organs shutting down. I could not come to grips with the fact that my wife of 27 years and mother of our two young adult boys could possibly die.

Nancy endured health issues for about fourteen years. We spent the first four years going to doctors and specialists, but nobody had a good answer or the ability to give us a diagnosis to act on. Over the years, she had been labeled with fibromyalgia, irritable bowel syndrome, and environmental sensitivities; she was tested for lupus, multiple sclerosis, Crohn's disease, and more. Nothing confirmed, no real diagnosis, and my wife's body was not responding. Given all the time and failures, I was giving up on the medical community.

This story is not unique to our family. There are so many suffering a multitude of challenges and afflictions. This is about *all* family members. The one suffering obviously needs help, but the rest of the family, the children, and the caregiver are also impacted in a huge way. When we married, we shared vows of "love and affection, in sickness and in health, until death do us part." I take those vows seriously and with conviction.

Faced with health issues, but still needing to raise our kids and hold down a full-time job to make ends meet, I was tested to, and beyond, my limits. We made it a priority to be involved with our boys: volunteering at their schools, coaching sports, and focusing on family activities. We did not want to be absentee parents.

But when Nancy got sick and was not able to participate the way we wanted to as a couple and a family, it was really hard. We were all together but she was physically not able to join in. Even meals together were hard. She was so sensitive we couldn't cook like we used to. So she would prepare for herself the limited foods that she could still tolerate while I either cooked outdoors on the grill or took the boys out to dinner without her.

It was by no means easy, but I was determined to find answers and make it work. All of my life I felt the need to be self-sufficient and independent, and to be successful in relationships, in school, or at work. It was on my shoulders (or so I thought). No one could do it but me. I was responsible to succeed or fail. I thought it was up to me. I thought I had to do it. *But God. . .* This book is a testimony of the power of prayer! Of a life-giving promise. What I learned personally on this journey is that once I gave my heart to the Lord and invited Jesus into my heart, now it was no longer about me. It was surrendering to God and understanding that He can carry the burden for me. And by partnering, by believing, and making the time to pray and learn, miracles can and do happen.

Our goal in putting this book together is to share a message of hope, and life, and promise. The Bible says to ask and it will be given to you, seek and you will find, knock and the door will be opened. Ask and you shall receive (Matthew 7:7–11). We want to impart this testimony to share that anyone can press in for their miracle healing as well. Freely God will give, if we believe and receive.

You are about to read my wife's recollections of successes and failures, highs and lows, and the ultimate answers and steps of faith that got her back to health and wellness, and our lives being renewed.

Read on. You will be amazed and, we hope, encouraged to find answers in your own life, and those of your family, your friends, and those that you come in contact with every day. This is a story of pain and brokenness miraculously redeemed by Jesus. Truly, beauty for ashes.

Richard Johnson

Husband of the author, and father of our two amazing sons.

Chapter 1

There is a Glorious Savior After All

*Fear not, for I have redeemed you; I have
called you by name. You are mine.*
—Isaiah 43:1

MY WORLD WAS spinning. All the life was being sucked out of my body, and try as I might, I couldn't hold it together anymore. I admitted to my husband I was freezing to death, alone in this huge new house on Camano Island, totally isolated from family and friends. This was a crucial moment for him, he had to talk some sense into me. Oh, how I knew the hospital was the last place in the world I wanted to go. But I was dying. No question about it. So he carried me to the car since I was beyond walking at this point. The last shreds of my will to hold on were being cut off. Was my case hopeless?

The diagnosis: I was suffering from years of malnutrition and now I had hypothermia with an 85-degree body core temperature. I would not survive unless they could get me warm and put me on an IV. I lost it all then. All my mind and memory went too. I was put on a hot bed and onto IV therapy at the hospital. After six days with them trying to keep me on the hot bed (apparently they say I could hardly stay on it), I was released to go home. When they put me on the IV, some unknown allergy produced an adverse effect on my brain. I lost all memory function on top of all the rest. At that point, I didn't know who I was or where I was.

In 1985, I started with a few pains here and there, and over many years of struggle, this was all I had left. I thought I had tried everything to get well. But by this point, I could barely walk, stand, or sit down. I was living in a bubble, very allergic to almost everything. For three of those years I could only eat two foods, cod and broccoli. By 2008, I was severely ill and could not tolerate the cold weather; I was literally freezing to death and I was so allergic I could not even get blankets over me and only one dress was tolerable.

We lived in Spokane, Washington with zero-degree temperatures being common in the winter. And I would go out every day and try to get in my car because I wasn't going to lose the battle. My car was my freedom and I had been homebound before, and so I had many fears of having to start all over again from scratch. The allergies made everything seem incredibly impossible and so hard in this lowest of places. My heart was totally bound up in walls of protection. But I clung to that car with all my willpower and I would not give up, freezing and sitting in it, crying, "If this is all I can do to go outside, I will do it!" And then in a last-ditch effort, we tried one more move to get me back out of the cold weather and into Western Washington.

After months of research, my husband and I discovered a drier area on Camano Island in the rain shadow of the Olympic Mountains. Hoping to stay out of the mold of the Northwest, we took a huge risk and moved me again, not knowing if I would tolerate the new house. Previous moves had already shown tremendous environmental sensitivities. Our oldest son had already moved out after a little college and our youngest son was staying behind to finish college in Spokane. It was all new and no one would be home with me while my husband was at work. Alone almost all day, lonely, and grieving about becoming empty-nesters, I went downhill fast.

After the episode in the hospital, my husband took me home and he said I did not know who he was. But he took care of me out of the goodness of his heart. And he took action to get me together with a naturopath near our home whom I had seen right before going to the hospital. She made some calls to a brain specialist and found a special fish oil that crossed the blood-brain barrier.

They started me on it right away. . . hoping to heal my brain.

Around 30 days later, I woke up all at once. All the memories came flooding back in. I remember it distinctly, I was sitting at a table eating. I saw what I was eating, and these were not foods I could tolerate. I looked up and saw my husband smiling at me. He recognized the look in my eyes. "Is that my Nancy?" But I jumped up and was pounding on his chest, saying, "What are you feeding me?" as all the fears came flooding back in. But he took hold of me and smiling, he told me the story of how he had been taking care of me and feeding me vitamins and new foods for over 30 days and I was doing fine with them. Wow! I was so grateful! It was a true gift from God not to be in control of my own care. My husband who is wonderful had done such a good job!

We continued to live on the edge with this small improvement. Watching TV one evening, my husband happened to switch onto a Joel Osteen church service. Rarely had we ever watched Christian sermons. He called me out to watch with him. It was called "A Night of Hope." I watched with burning interest as this pastor poured out such hope in God's miracles and told about the lives that were changed. He told so many stories of healings and how prayer really worked. My heart soared with hope and the desire to be well and I was thrilled by his messages. There was an excitement in me and a pounding in my heart I had not known before. Emotions flooded over me. Oh my goodness, could this be my chance? *Could I ask God for a miracle?* I really felt like this man was telling the truth about Jesus and that miracles were real. I had prayed the Lord's prayer many times and had others praying for me but this was different. They were talking about having relationship with Jesus. They called it "being born again."

Someone had asked me about being born again years before, but I never really knew what it meant. I thought it was something religious. We were not involved in church at all. My husband and I had walked away from the church when we moved to Spokane, not finding one that fit us. I was raised Catholic and my husband Lutheran. But this was about relationship and I was completely broken, without hope of any kind. I had hardly anything left of myself and no answers. And I wanted to live! I had dreams for myself and my husband and family. I knew there was something here! I could feel a huge excitement in my weak body. There had to be an answer.

Even though I had studied over 100 self-help books, and tried every type of doctor and healer, I never found a solution to what would really heal my spirit, soul, or body. A few times I rebounded a little but never got healed. But by the third Sunday of watching Joel Osteen, I found out what the deepest cry of my heart was. It was *Jesus* and His promise of salvation and hope. He was going to bring me real hope. And hoping in Him meant maybe, just maybe, I had a chance of getting well beyond my wildest imagination and more.

So I stepped up and asked Jesus into my heart at the end of the show. After years of searching with a lost heart, longing for something better, it was Jesus I had needed all along. And I was aware of my heart when Jesus came in, and I saw darkness fly out and His light come streaming in. Then I heard a voice that wasn't mine, saying: "I thought you wanted to be God. . .?" Wow! That was somehow familiar to me, but yet it wasn't. It was not me and it was not God. Was I freaking out! Three weeks later, my husband also said the same prayer with Jesus. And it was the beginning of our process of building a real relationship with this amazing God named Jesus. Not religion, but Jesus as our friend and savior.

So passionately did God love me (and the world) that He sent His only Son that I might have eternal life (John 3:16). Not only did He want me to have eternal life in heaven and no longer be a slave to sin, but He wanted me to live a full and healthy life on earth: actually heaven on earth! I found out there were incredible promises God made in the Bible to His people. And He wanted me to pray to Him and ask for them. I had known there was a God and that I could pray to Him. But I never really had a relationship with the living God.

The good news of the gospel tells all of us who have sinned and are sick or in poverty that we are forgiven and washed clean of all of it. He died and went to the cross for the worst of sinners because He *loved* us. That's where I was. Totally at the bottom, the worst place, with no hope. And God—you could say *Love*—isn't holding anything against us; he's canceled it all out. And we are completely washed white as snow and free of all shame, condemnation, and guilt. If we don't know this, we could go to hell even though all our debts are already canceled (Colossians 2:13–15). We just need to be born again. It is that simple.

I was raised Catholic and went along praying the Lord's Prayer, but only achieving limited success with it. I didn't know that God was love. I had a Catholic priest when I was young but didn't understand the Bible or the New Testament and its promises. But Joel Osteen was saying that I could ask God (who is love) to do the impossible according to His Word and I could stand firm on it and believe He would do it. Wow! That was mind-blowing. A God who was "my" God who would promise me victory. When Jesus died on the cross, His whole intent was to take my sin upon Himself, give me eternal life, and heal me by His stripes, past, present, and future (1 Peter 2:24). It is a fantastic exchange for anyone who will accept Him and I jumped all the way in, all of me for all of Him!

But that is not all. The deeper truth that the church seems to have lost over the years, is that Jesus intends to live in us, and when He comes in, He makes us new creations (2 Corinthians 5:17) and will heal everything, if we just ask. And it gets better: He intends for us to live life and life to the fullest. A life like heaven on earth. He wants us totally set free to live a supernatural life with Him in our hearts and at our side, in *limitless* blessings. Supernatural beings. Invited into divine union with God. Oh, my goodness! This is fantastically good news! He finished it all at the cross about 2000 years ago. And it is only as we believe and receive this amazing truth, that we will have the victory!

So my head was on overload. But I knew that I had to learn the truth really fast if I was going to survive. Everything I had been taught about the source of sickness was wrong. I had no idea that I had an enemy (satan) who was trying to kill me (John 10:10). It was not natural causes! All those doctor reports were not the real truth. That sick person was not me. I would have to let go of those old beliefs fast and start believing the promises of healing in the Bible. Since I was allergic to all medications, I had zero options in the natural world. But here was a chance! I was going to have to pursue this truth with all of my heart.

Nearly dead, with no hope, I put all my trust in Jesus. I had to read the Bible and understand what was going on here. Originally, there was no sickness on the earth in the Garden of Eden, and there is certainly no sickness in heaven either. The enemy was the one making me sick and I had come into agreement with it. Not only that, but I found out that there were certain spiritual laws that would govern my life if I could get a hold of them. The truth was starting to crack the years of wrong mindsets and the hardness of my heart. Why had no one ever told me?

Step 1

The first miracle I discovered was getting into a relationship with Jesus and inviting Him to come live in my heart. His very essence is love, the kind of love you would never want to miss for a moment! I would be dead today if it wasn't for Him. It's the best decision I have ever made. He is real, He is alive, and He is full of life-giving love and joy. He can walk you through your healing and into your future destiny. He has turned my life into a miracle story of hope and love. And He will do that for you too.

Next, I had to be willing to be healed and willing to change. After I learned Jesus could do miracles, I had to fight for my life with Him. That was the key. I had to be willing to ask Jesus to help me. After I accepted Him, He made me brand-new and gave me eternal life. I was able to come out of the past and step forward into my future destiny. Today I walk out an amazing life with an amazing God who helps me with everything and does good to me every day. It's fantastically fun and adventurous and overflowing with joy. He is my everything. And now I am no longer just human, but full of power and love. It's called being a new creation. So if you have not invited Jesus into your heart, this is the first step to your salvation and healing. It is critical to where your spirit is going to go for eternity. I urge you to come home to your Father in heaven. It is a matter of life or death, heaven or hell. I said this simple prayer:

Prayer for salvation: Beautiful Jesus, come into my heart, I believe in you and that you are the Son of God. Forgive me of all my sins, lead and guide me through life, be my Father, and fill me with your loving Holy Spirit. In the name of Jesus, amen.

Chapter 2

You Are the Apple of God's Eye

You will also be [considered] a crown of
glory and splendor in the hand of the LORD,
And a royal diadem [exceedingly beautiful]
in the hand of your God.
—Isaiah 62:3

CAUGHT IN HORRIBLE night terrors for years,
I knew of a spirit realm and it wasn't a good one.
I was tormented and hardly sleeping. It was very
real, very dark, and very scary. I dreaded going to
bed at night and would surround my bed with my
attempted prayers of protection. After trying chi-
ropractors, naturopaths, and acupuncturists, I
moved on to new-age healers, reiki masters, spirit
healers, muscle testing, aromatherapy, crystals,
and other new-age techniques. And this search to
get well no matter the cost, actually opened me up
to truths that seemed fine at the time, but were
dark. And I just kept getting worse.

But now Jesus was asking me to trust Him when I had taken care of myself for years, and even though it was misguided, it was all I knew. Because God is a Spirit too, I was uncertain and I didn't know how to trust Him. But I had read somewhere about asking God to come and make Himself known to you at night. So I prayed for that and went to bed and waited in the quiet to see what would happen. And to my surprise, the sweetest presence of Jesus came to me that night and He spoke comforting words of safety! And I was convinced then it was a battle between good and evil. And Jesus wanted my heart, He wanted to love me. And He was winning!

From then on I would pray and ask Jesus to hold me all night because He cared about protecting me. And I also found out God is faithful to His word. There was a verse that was prayed over me again and again at the Healing Rooms. So I prayed it at night:

The beloved of the Lord shall dwell in safety by Him, Who shelters him all the day long. And he shall dwell between His shoulders.
                    —Deuteronomy 33:12

And God would hold me right between His shoulders and every time I would wake up through the night, He was still holding me in his great arms of loving kindness. Eventually, I could fall asleep without fear and was healed of those dreams.

I had never seen myself through Love's eyes—God's eyes—before. Eyes that beheld the beauty of His beloved. Could I receive that? I had condemned and rejected myself for so many years: the way I felt and looked so sick. But the Bible said I was wonderful and worthy to receive His love and that I actually ravished the heart of God. Check out this verse:

> You have ravished My heart, My sister, *My* spouse; you have ravished My heart with one *look* of your eyes, with one link of your necklace.
>
> —Song of Solomon 4:9

I was a chosen jewel of immanent worth. And so are you. We can be defined as having great merit, character, or value, people of commendable excellence, who are deserving and worthy of receiving. This is what Jesus thinks about all of us. Absolutely royal. Brand-new creations, the Bible says, having Christ living in us.

I started feeling His different perspective even though my soul was still all bound up behind walls of brokenness. I would feel a sweet love around me—He cared about everything in my life! He would talk to me about doing things I couldn't do. He knew that I could do those things that seemed impossible to me. He had a thousand thoughts about me and *all* of them were good. He was speaking to me in a still, small voice saying that He believed in me. I was very restricted with allergies but He helped me. It was a soft voice in the chatter of a tortured mind. But it was there.

Jesus was helping me. Even though I had felt so unloved, fearful, abandoned, and alone without any relief, I was slowly warming up. My Savior was fighting for me to hear and to know that I was loved; He actually cherished me, like the apple of His eye. I was treasured and adored by Jesus.

Two years after our wedding, my husband, who had never seen me cry before, was at a loss for words. As a young mother, I had started to get sick and then got worse and worse. But I just couldn't pretend anymore: something was really wrong with me. My life was consumed with trying to get well and at the same time be a mother, wife, and daughter. I had one beautiful baby boy and then another one just as adorable almost five years later. My husband was amazing and it had seemed like I was in control of my life. But the illness took over and became my identity. When the doctors had no answer, I had to fight for my own healthcare. And slowly I slid into a downward spiral of believing the lie that I would never recover.

But where there had been total hopelessness, now there was this loving voice of Jesus saying: "You are my friend and you are my bride. I have made a covenant agreement with you to be your God and to answer your prayers." And I would see myself differently for a minute through the haze. Jesus would lead me to read a Christian book, or watch a Christian program on TV. And I could feel God come into the room. And I started to get educated. And wow, did I have a lot to learn! But the simplicity of Jesus is love. He loved me and He knew how to heal me. And every day there would be some small victory that I could never have done without Him. He led me through fearful allergy situations. With such severe allergies, even a small hurdle like switching to new towels or getting a new dress was a huge ordeal for me. I never knew God loved me and cared about even the smallest details of my life. But He proved it to me over and over again.

Simple pleasures like having a pet, or flowers on the counter, were out of the question. But Jesus gave me flowers! One day in the spring of my healing, He showed me some tiny delicate daffodils in our garden at the new house. He encouraged me to pick them. I intended they would have to sit outside and I could look at them through the window. But no, He encouraged me to bring them in. They were so tiny, I thought, "Okay, Lord even though I am afraid of allergic reactions, I am just going to follow your heart because You want me to have them." And I did it, and there was no reaction! I was really getting healed. It was okay and I felt so adored by Jesus that He wanted to give me flowers, and not only that, He gave me the courage I needed to bring them in. I cried with gratitude that I might be able to be normal again. It meant the world to me.

No matter what kind of mistakes or sin we have gotten mixed up in, or what we have done, or what we are trying to hide from Him, God wants us as His very own beloved. Why? Because we are made for love. To be loved, and to love. We are the crowning glory of His creation, His beautiful children and the bride of Christ. Isn't that amazing? In the beginning, God created everything, but the last thing He did before He rested was to say: "Let us create man in our own image" (Genesis 1:26). So we have been made in His glorious image. And He intends for us to walk in that revelation. It means that we are meant for royalty. We are divine sons and daughters of God. When we get saved, we are adopted into the royal family and into the bloodline of Christ. God intended for us to live, move, and have our being within Him and to walk with Him as His very own children of love (Acts 17:28).

We are the apple of His eye. And He never takes His beautiful eyes off of us. He wants us to be in constant communion with Him and to enjoy and take delight in His nature and His ways. His great plan was for His children to display His glory, His nature, and His love. We are also to multiply so that we can take dominion over the earth and be fruitful in every way. All for a God who is nothing but good. Wow! When Jesus came to earth, He defeated satan by taking on a body, dying for our sins, and then being buried and resurrected. He did not come to condemn us. He did not come to make us feel guilty. He did not come to blame us. He came to put us back into intimate relationship with a Father of *Love*. Everything He has, He has given to us as His beloved. And everything we are, we give to Him. He meant it as a magnificent exchange. We have a brand-new identity, and we have overcome the world

32

with Him. The identity I had taken on, as a victim of sickness, did not belong to me. That sick person was not me. I was, and we are, such priceless treasures to God that He paid the highest price: the sacrifice of His very own Son to get us back. You are absolutely priceless.

So with Jesus invited into my heart, I was now no longer just human. And when you do this, neither are you. We are a temple of the Holy Spirit Himself. God's heart for us is to have victory over sickness and sin in our lives on earth as well as eternal life in heaven. And we are priceless indeed. God adopts us and calls us His very own children. He even makes us citizens of heaven and invites us into His family. He is our very own Father. Not only that, He calls us Kings and Priests and we will rule and reign on this earth (Revelation 5:10). He gives us complete access to Him in prayer and we are being prepared to become just like Jesus. That is off-the-charts good news! Literally, as Jesus is, so are we on this earth. We are as powerful and as lovely as Jesus, with the same Spirit (1 John 4:17). He equips us and prepares us so that we can heal others and share His truth. Not only are we treasured, loved unconditionally, and highly prized by the Father, but we are betrothed to Jesus. And we are co-creators and co-heirs with Him in the Kingdom of God.

The Father who created us wants us to also love and appreciate ourselves and others. Because He made us, we are made of love. The most prized commandment in Scripture is to love God with all your heart, and love your neighbor as yourself (Mark 12:29–31). We fall in love with our Heavenly Father and we find out what that love is like. Then we can love ourselves with His love and eventually move on to our neighbors. He wants us to see that we are good. This is what I found hard to do. Because I had so much fear and sin in my life, I was punishing myself and condemning myself. And I would never forgive myself. But God said no, you must forgive yourself and love everything about yourself. You must appreciate every feature about yourself. Your body is beautiful, your mind is beautiful, your emotions are beautiful, and your spirit is beautiful. Even your life, with all its pain (even though He didn't cause it) has been beautiful to Him because He has seen it through the eyes of love.

He has never stopped believing the best about you. His is a love that never stops seeing your full and beautiful potential. A love that can and will turn everything for good to those who love Him and are called to His purpose (Romans 8:28).

In a worship service one time, He took me back on a journey through all my negative memories from birth to that day. He showed me in every case where I had trauma, deception, addictions, pain, disease, or devastation, that He was there and He did *not* condemn me. He was with me speaking love and life to me, and encouraging me to make the right choices. He loved me through it all. He was right in front of me the whole time and He was looking at me with a love that longed to be received. But I never perceived Him. I was so lost and deceived that I never reached out to Him. As I realized the ramifications of His unrelenting love, I cried and cried for the sweetness of His good heart. He told me that all the good things that had happened to me through my life were from Him. All those bad things were from the enemy and that I had come into agreement with them because He made me with a will to choose my own way. But Love stood steadfastly by my side, waiting for the day I would cry out to Him with all my heart.

I know that we all need to take a fresh look at ourselves in the mirror and see the beauty that He has made. We need to see all the good in our lives and forgive ourselves. We are unique. We are one of a kind and there is no one else on this earth who has our fingerprints. He cries out to love us personally and to receive our personal love for Him. He loves to be loved and so do we. Only our love will complete and fulfill His heart. We came from His heart and He created us with the greatest of love. When we love Him in return, He is delighted to pour out on us blessings greater than we can imagine.

God has as many thoughts toward us as the number of grains of sand on the seashore (Psalm 139:17–18). That's a lot of good thoughts toward our total well-being. When we ask Him to help us love ourselves unconditionally without judgment, we will see how our body and mind respond. See yourself with God's eyes of love. Challenge yourself to look at and appreciate every detail of yourself in the mirror for 30 days. Our bodies, minds, and spirits thrive on love! God loves Himself and He can teach us how to love ourselves too.

Step 2

In this step, Jesus taught me that one of the miracles is all about my identity. He asked me one day, "Do you know you are royal, my darling? You have rights as a child of God, you have been adopted, and your past has been wiped clean." This is what the enemy said to Jesus in the desert, "If you are the son of God, then. . ." in several different ways. But Jesus *knew* who He was. He *knew* it deep in His heart as He spent His life gazing upon the Father and it could not be taken from Him. You also are no longer an orphan, but have been adopted as God's child.

Prayer for the revelation of my true identity: Father, I pray that You would give me a revelation that I am the apple of Your eye and that I am Your royal son or daughter. Thank you that I am literally Your masterpiece and the crowning glory of Your creation, a royal diadem in Your hand. Show me that I am worthy to receive you. I want to see myself the way you see me; adopted, powerful, righteous, glorious, chosen, holy, and unconditionally loved. And I want to love myself the way you love me. In the name of Jesus, amen.

Chapter 3

Forgiveness Once and For All

Farther than from a sunrise to a sunset—
that's how far you've removed our guilt
from us. The same way a loving father
feels toward his children—that's but a
sample of your tender feelings toward us,
your beloved children,
who live in awe of you.
—Psalm 103:12–14 (TPT)

GOD'S INFINITE MERCY never comes to an end. And it's new every morning. Every morning, every night, and even every moment, He has a gift of mercy for us. Compassion and grace flow out of Him continuously. He is a Dad who will stand us back up over and over again until we make it around the mountain.

I had almost died twice, and the last time, I had become so weak that I finally surrendered every last bit of control and let go and let God. I humbled myself before God and He poured on the grace. Because I didn't understand that God had forgiven me, not to mention that I needed to forgive myself, my body was suffering horribly. When I just couldn't seem to get well, a victim mentality settled in and so did the voice of the enemy. My beautiful spiritual inner child was hidden beneath pride, fear, condemnation, and self-determination. It was a downward spiral. But God had forgiven me completely *and* He never condemned me. As a matter of fact, He had placed it all in His vast sea of forgetfulness and didn't even remember it anymore. It was shocking, but God was not reminding me of my past; He had forgotten all about it. Yay! Wow! What an amazing idea.

For years I had read psychology books that talked about forgiveness, so I decided on my own to forgive everyone and release all my family members. But the hardest person to forgive was me. I was completely ignorant of the enemy's assignment to destroy me with his accusations. In the Healing Rooms, the first thing they ask people with long-standing illnesses is if they have someone they need to forgive. It's a major stumbling block to healing because unforgiveness will cover the heart so that we can't receive from God. After a few times of interviewing me, they finally got to the issue. You have forgiven everyone else, but do you understand that God forgives you, and will you forgive yourself?

My heart broke wide open and I truly forgave myself of a life of weakness, with the help of some real prayer warriors agreeing with me. There were huge sobs coming out of me. "Yes, I forgive myself and release myself." I had become the judge and I had bitterness and anger. And there was such a stronghold of condemnation that to believe it completely, I had to confess many times daily, "God forgives me, and I forgive myself." After three months of confessing this, I finally received the revelation of God's sweet mercies and forgiveness deep inside of me.

Since I wasn't in relationship with Jesus before, I didn't know His great, big, unconditionally loving nature. He wants us to feel safe, valued, connected, nourished, protected, and understood. He also wants us to know that He accepts us right where we are and that we don't have to be perfect. I had wanted to be excellent, but Jesus was telling me just to do my best and I could learn as I went without having to perform for His love and acceptance. Then I realized He really liked me! Wow! And so He taught me to love myself, and my beautiful inner child, and to forgive myself. He will do this with you too.

I read a story once about a dog who had been chained up for years. Well, they took the chain off the dog but he never ran free. Why? Because he didn't believe it. It's sad, but he had been chained and bound up for so long he never made the connection and never tested it out. As believers, we have been washed clean of every sin. If you are punishing yourself, let the past go. That old man has died and was buried at the cross. We are now the righteousness of God in Christ Jesus and have full access to stand before the throne of God. We are innocent, clean, pure, and beautiful in His sight. We are truly and absolutely free and without spot or wrinkle in our spirits.

In prayer and worship one time, I was lying down, trying to understand God's love for me, when I saw His huge hand come down out of heaven and pick me up. I felt like I shot up like a rocket somewhere really high. I was like a tiny doll in His huge, loving hand and He clutched me next to His beating heart of love. He squeezed me so tightly with love, I thought my bones would break. But I just melted in His love. And I tried to explain that I had done this and that, and I wasn't worthy of such extravagant love. And He said, with tears in His eyes that He didn't care about the mistakes I had made; He just wanted to love me. And His love was jealous for me. I cried and cried with Him as He hugged me tight. I couldn't run anymore from His captivating love. He loved me all the way through, inside and out. He loved everything about me and He wanted me to know it.

We have to be vulnerable enough to allow Him to love us! And we have to be humble enough to come and ask for it in prayer. His love is the most healing and comforting experience we will ever know. He absolutely adores us. Over and over He said He didn't care about my mistakes. He just wanted to love me. I could feel His longing and all His endless patience in that fierce love. Finally, I was receiving it. I laid there for hours receiving and soaking in His love, like a sponge.

With other people, family or friends, it is the same. God calls us to forgive each other before the sun goes down, and if we have anything against our brother to go and make it right (Ephesians 4:25–32). We need to always choose to keep our love on. If we are walking in the high calling of love towards God, ourselves, and others, we won't even think to hold onto anger or bitter-root judgments. Because Jesus forgave us of everything at the cross, He wants us to forgive others too. Forgiveness is an act of our will and our emotions. It's a decision we make. It does not deny or justify the offense. It does not mean the person who committed the offense is not responsible for their actions before God and civil laws. And it does not always mean reconciliation either. Here are some of the symptoms of unforgiveness: deception, betrayal, hatred, confusion, disbelief, disappointment, blaming others, and bitterness.

Pride will also cause us to believe we are superior to others, and when pride comes, then comes disgrace (Proverbs 11:2). We must take time regularly to see the true condition of our heart and be grateful and thankful for our lives and the people around us. If we are walking in love and forgiveness, we won't hold things against God, ourselves, or our brothers (2 Timothy 2:22–26). He doesn't want us to hide or isolate ourselves or the enemy will eat our lunch and pop the bag, too. This is what I did for years. Be up front, honest, and humbly repent if needed. God is good and already knows all of our inner struggles anyway. We must face what's wrong and take responsibility for our lives.

Definition of forgiveness: a conscious, deliberate decision to release feelings of resentment or vengeance toward a person or group who has harmed you, regardless of whether or not they have actually asked for forgiveness.

If we want to be powerful people, we must give others mercy and grace and choose to build healthy relationships with strong connections. This is what I am still learning, but God is teaching me to get up every day and share the love in my heart with others. And I praise God for opening up my heart to love again. I cried such tears of relief, "Oh, how sweet it is to love others!" Just one moment in a tender embrace. . . We must open our hearts to love others and build intimate connections. I have learned that I need to pursue intimate relationships; they don't pursue me. It took a lot of courage for me to be willing to know others and to be known by them. But after all those years of devastating loneliness, I have finally been able to open my heart to a deeper marriage and deeper friendships. And I have fallen in love all over again with my husband and with my friends and family. As Christians, this is how we are to be known: by our love for each other.

God helped me to be willing to accept people the way they are and to seek for the gold inside of them instead of judging. Looking at myself, I too have many faults, perhaps more than others. If we are not willing to forgive, we will leave a foothold for the enemy and give him the right to come in and cause sickness. Many of us tend to isolate ourselves because of offense. But when we forgive, the spirit that is tormenting us no longer has any rights. It has to leave, and a healing is released!

I went round and round like a hamster on a wheel, never finding the solution and totally focused on the problem. That is exactly the enemy's plan, to have us focus all our attention on him, and to have us so deceived and confused that we can't untangle ourselves. But God has the answer. And it is not years and years of counseling. No! No! But how? Because you have been crucified with Jesus, you no longer live, and now you live by the faith of the Son of God (Galatians 2:20). What that means is that we are now living in Christ and we have His heart (mind, will, emotions) and His Spirit, yet still retain our own authentic personality. We don't have to go through years of healing. We can receive it today if we renew our mind to it, know it, and believe it.

I was laying on my bed one day and I was visualizing cutting all the dead branches off the tree of my life. And Jesus walked up to me and said: "No, let's just chop that tree down. I don't want to fix you; I have made you brand-new!" And you know, He is right. So celebrate! We are a brand-new creation that is alive to God, and we have been set free of satan's control. Our job now is to learn about who we are and what we have as God's children. So just believe it. It's a switch in perspective. God said it, and He is not a man that He should lie (Numbers 23:19).

Step 3

So I learned to humbly receive God's awesome mercies and forgiveness. And I learned to forgive myself and others, let offense go, and get up and be well again. God has an amazing purpose for my life and He has one for you too. Open hearts of radiant love and mercy are the miracle. Grow in seeing the gold in yourself and in others, because we are all God's unique expressions and His dreams come true. We are pure and beautiful in His sight and we are to be a light to this world. If we have Jesus in us, we have it all! Bob Jones, a powerful man of God, went to heaven and God said: "Did you learn to love?" He said, "No." And God sent him back and gave him another chance. Choose to love and forgive today. Please pray this prayer:

Prayer for forgiveness: Father, I humbly receive your gracious forgiveness. I ask you to forgive me for holding onto offense against you, others, or even myself. As an act of my will and by your grace, I choose to forgive myself and to release myself for all my sins. As an act of my will

and by your grace, I also choose to forgive
_____ and I release this person
in every way for what he or she did to me. I ask
you to separate the sin away from this person and
nail it to the cross. I release this person into your
hands and pray for your mercy to be upon him or
her. I choose to release blessings! Please heal my
wounded emotions and memories, and give me
your grace to treat myself and this person well in
every way. Thank you for giving me the power to
walk in your love. I forgive myself and this person
like you have forgiven me. Please show me anyone else I need to forgive and release. Thank you
for washing and cleansing us in the blood of
Jesus. In the name of Jesus, amen.

Chapter 4

The Living Word of Truth

Not one promise from God is empty of
power, for nothing is impossible with God!
—Luke 1:37 (TPT)

WE DIE FOR lack of knowledge (Hosea 4:6).
And that is exactly what was happening with me.
I didn't know that God healed, or that He had
promises in the Bible. One morning I woke up
and couldn't believe my eyes. There was a supernatural rainbow on display in my bedroom over
my bed. I thought it was a dream, but I was
awake and I could see it with my eyes open or
closed. It was stunning, awesome, and very bril-
liant. Eventually I had to stop staring at it, and
go about my day. And I never saw it again. Oh,
the colors were glorious! A few days later I found
out in the Bible, the rainbow was God's sign to
Noah that He had made a covenant promise to
him. "I set My rainbow in the cloud, and it shall
be for the sign of the covenant between Me and

the earth" (Genesis 9:13). A covenant is like an agreement, contract, or guarantee.

If God wanted me to be sure of His promises, He had just done an extraordinary miracle. I never forgot it. And I was thrilled with Him! I didn't know I had a covenant with Him, where I exchanged my life for His, and where He promised with all His integrity to do good to me and to show Himself strong for me. Wow! I went to work reading the New Testament eagerly and finding out my new identity and His promises. I needed to eat, sleep, and live what the Bible says because in John 8:32 it explains, when you know the truth, the truth will set you free. There was no time to waste. Since I now had Jesus inside me, I needed to train myself to know who He was, and what He could do, and who I was, and what I could do.

But I was utterly lost in the belief systems that agreed with the world and the enemy, and I was caught, like many, in a trap of deception and lies. Our enemy satan is called the father of lies. For years and years I had listened to a familiar spirit speaking lies thinking it was my body talking, but not so. Until we realize there are only two minds, the mind of Christ (that thinks the word of Truth) and the mind of satan, we are vulnerable to being deceived. We are called to cast down those arguments and to bring them into captivity to the obedience of Christ (2 Corinthians 10:4–6).

When I could find no answers with doctors, I searched out Naturopathic doctors, acupuncture, and new-age healers to get relief. Counseling really never helped at all. I read over 100 self-help books, looking everywhere for healing. Everywhere except really listening to the conviction inside my heart or getting in the Bible.

The disease they labeled me with was called "fibromyalgia." It manifested itself in all-over body pain, but it was mostly pain in my face. In the beginning of the fibromyalgia, they hooked me up to a biofeedback machine and taught me to control pain with my mind. I had meditation tapes for relaxation and used visualizations of peaceful scenes. The meditation worked only as long as I was doing it. Then the pain would return.

But meditation was a huge mistake for me. Since I started to receive some relief as I did it, I then began to study it further. I moved into transcendental meditation and then into Buddhist meditation, not realizing the dangers of an empty mind: it opens the door to the demonic. Once that type of meditation was established in my mind by the deception of the enemy, I easily moved into trying to find out if new-age healers could help me. I went to their fairs, searching for the latest in healing. As a last-ditch effort to get well, I even went out of the country to a new-age healing retreat. I knew there were people experimenting with witchcraft and trying to find power outside themselves and something of a demonic realm, but I was clueless about the enemy's plans to steal, kill, and destroy people with sickness. He literally wants to kill you (see John 10:10). And it's very real. Don't get involved in the new-age practices. They are loaded with demonically in-spired doctrines, spiritual darkness, and death. I want to give a strong warning and say it again, *stay out of the new age.* I almost died because I was not informed. But we are in a very real spir-itual battle and it's the light against the dark.

God asked me to join the Healing Room prayer team and my progress continued at an even greater speed as I prayed for others, and hope was brought back into my life and theirs. I was living again and smiling and laughing and realizing that God could do anything when you really went after it and believed in Him. Wow! I was really loved by God. *He really loved me!* And He was just like the Jesus in the Bible, healing everyone. It is His nature to heal. You can't get near Him without getting healed. Much of what went on with me (and also with others I prayed for), was listening to the *lying* symptoms that had become such a fa-miliar voice. I watched many people get their healings right away and some kept coming back. It was the ones who were really hungry, repen-tant, and at the end of themselves, who changed rapidly in the Lord's Healing Presence.

It is also a real battle of the mind. I had to steadfastly refuse to listen to the lies, the past, to the victim mentality, and I had to take that healing by force. I had to go for it with all my heart. I had to be radical! There was an enemy who wanted to kill me. As a baby Christian, I was learning the truth of God's living word, my identity, my author-ity over the enemy, and about daily confessing the

Word of God out loud. God was doing His part, and I had to do mine and keep my mind filled with good thoughts of health and wholeness.

The most important thing for us to learn is the truth of God's Word. He has given it to us like a Last Will and Testament and it is medicine to our spirits, souls, and bodies. It is like a manual for living. It is our birthright and our identity is in Christ. If your identity is a person who will never get well, or has to stay on drugs your whole life, then that is what will happen. But God wants to enlighten our mind with His promises and the truth. And it is the truth that will set us free. He is a Healer and He wants us well today. If we are born again, the work is already finished at the cross and it's in our born-again spirit. We just need to renew our mind to the truth and our body will come into agreement (Romans 12:1–2). We need to say yes!

All God's promises are yes and amen (2 Corinthians 1:20). He says yes and we say amen! The Holy Spirit is our teacher. He will be the one to open the Word of God to us and teach us how to feed our spirits. As we eat from the tree of life, Jesus, the Word of God, it will work effectually in those who believe (1 Thessalonians 2:13). So we need to let Him highlight a healing promise to us, then we can meditate on it. Go over and over it. When we meditate, we take a verse and say it out loud, read it, and pray over it for a revelation. And we ask God questions to pull all the secrets out of it. And He will help us embrace that promise and it will become so real that it will drown out any other thought. It finally starts to burn inside. God's supernatural, living word starts washing away all the old thinking, allowing the promise to manifest in us. Once we stop believing the lies, the sickness will have to go.

> Listen carefully, my dear child, to everything that I teach you, and pay attention to all that I have to say. Fill your thoughts with my words until they penetrate deep into your spirit. Then, as you unwrap my words, they will impart true life and radiant health into the very core of your being. So above all, guard the affections of your heart, for they affect all that you are. Pay attention to the welfare of your innermost being, for from there flows the wellspring of life.
> —Proverbs 4:20–23 (TPT)

It's a whole new and incredibly powerful way of thinking, based on the Word of God. When we get our healing, we will need to keep it. Negative thinking and concentrating on the symptoms and what's wrong will actually cause it to flare up. For years I read all the wrong books; all about natural health remedies and doctor reports, trying to help myself get well. This actually made it harder! I had to drop all of it and ask for God to rewrite the thinking patterns in my mind. So keep the truth before yourself constantly and your destiny will be transformed.

We also need to hear the healing Word constantly because it will build our faith. Faith comes by hearing, and hearing by the Word of God

(Romans 10:17). So another good thing to do is to listen to anointed healing ministers and get a revelation of healing. I recommend Andrew Wommack (awmi.net). When we keep getting it inside us, we will start to believe. Once we have it deep inside us, it can't be taken from us because it has become part of us.

Not only do we need to hear other ministers, but we need to hear our own voice speaking it because our confession will activate our faith. As long as it is Scriptural, God calls us to pray, say, thank, and do that Word. The key is *when* we speak the Word, first, we must believe it in our hearts and not doubt it, and second, have no unforgiveness against anyone. So we speak to the mountain of sickness and it has to go.

> For assuredly, I say to you, whoever says to this mountain, 'Be removed and be cast into the sea,' and does not doubt in his heart, but believes that those things he says will be done, he will have whatever he says. Therefore I say to you, whatever things you ask when you pray, believe that you receive *them,* and you will have *them.*
>
> —Mark 11:23–24

Our bodies will respond to our voice. It has been created to serve us. God created the world in the beginning by saying "let there be light" (Genesis 1:3). And since we are sons and daughters of God and have the Holy Spirit, we too can co-create with God by speaking out what we want. Everything God created, He created with words.

So we should never again be saying that we are sick. Charles Capps says: "You are not to be moved by what you see or feel. Be moved by *what the word says*. Say only *what the word says*. *The word says it will work out*. Stand on that." He also said that God told him: "I have told my people they can have what they say, but my people are saying what they have." We need to say: I am healed by the stripes of Jesus and believe it in our hearts. We should always say what we mean, and mean what we say. So if we start sowing the seeds of health and wellbeing, we will reap a harvest. The word of God is incorruptible, and once we speak it, it has to reap a harvest. And seed that is sown on good soil and open hearts will yield a harvest of 30, 60, and even 100 fold (Mark 4:13–20). Also whoever sows those words generously will reap generously.

There are other promises about speaking too. God's Word will not return to Him void but it will accomplish what He pleases (Isaiah 55:11). Wow! That's powerful. See the Appendix for a list of Who You Are in Christ, Faith Scriptures, and Healing Scriptures for you to confess and possess. You say them with faith, believing they are already done. I really had to spend some time on this in the beginning, but I finally started to get it memorized and down in my heart more and more. Even today, I still speak out my confessions regularly. The word of God is alive and active, sharper than any double-edged sword. . . (Hebrews 4:12). Are you using your sword to create what you want? What is your sound? Is it the sound of life or death? *Let glorious words come out of us!*

> The tongue has the power of life and death,
> and those who love it will eat its fruit.
>
> —Proverbs 18:21

Step 4

God promises us! We have His miraculous Word now to rely on, not our opinions. The sense realm has no control over us. He showed me the best way to think is to have no opinions! He said, "You've got my Word on it, Nancy." Our omnipotent Jesus came like a lightning bolt into this world as the Word of God. He is alive as the Word made flesh inside of you. So I had to commit to keeping the Word before me, speaking it, and believing in it. I had to think about what I was thinking about and retrain my thoughts that were like deep tracks in my brain. Choose life, not death. Agree with the promises and train yourself to push out negative thoughts.

Prayer to know God's supernatural Word: Father, help me to hunger to know your Word and all that it promises. I desire to be radically transformed by the renewal of my mind and to get your Word deep into my heart so that I will not be moved by what I see or feel. Help me to set my mind on heavenly things and to retrain my thinking habits. Also, Father, teach me to know the power of your Word on my lips. I want to co-create with you, Father, so I will take care to speak life like you do and believe that I can have what I say. In the name of Jesus, amen.

Chapter 5

You Have Authority Over Sickness

*Jesus summoned together his twelve apos-
tles and imparted to them authority over
every demon and the power
to heal every disease.*
—Luke 9:1

SICKNESS, GET OUT! That's right! Your new
identity is a powerful child of God and you can tell
sickness where to go. I had never heard of such
a thing as having authority over the enemy (who
caused the sickness) and my own body. But at
the Healing Rooms they told me again and again,
"You have authority over symptoms." So I started
telling sickness to get out. And you can too.

You have a position and a seating in Christ in
the heavenlies as a child of God (Ephesians 2:4–
6). And as I kept diligent watch over my thoughts,
I witnessed Jesus work within me. And I got

miraculously healed little by little. I stopped taking two naps a day right away. I had energy again. Previously because of the chronic fatigue syndrome, I had been sleeping 12 hours a night and taking three naps a day. All the pain of the fibromyalgia disappeared. One day it was totally gone. I had such tremendous inner-ear pain that I could not even listen to the radio. But I got my music back on. I couldn't drive at night because of night blindness, but now I don't have it. It all just left. I began to live this new life by faith and to trust God and His Word. And I kept getting better and better. He was making me beautiful inside and out.

There was a time when I had started at a ministry school and the winter temperatures started dropping below 35 degrees. It was getting very cold and I could still only wear a dress and sandals outside for the Friday outreaches. I tried to get out of it, but we all had to go. So I went in the bathroom and cried. I was freezing, but I was determined to do it by faith, hoping that Jesus would keep me warm. I still could not get pants around my waist because of severe eczema and dermatitis.

So I went the next Sunday and had a pastor pray and agree with me. I explained to him that God sent me to this school so I *had* to have proper clothes to wear. I really felt that the Lord would take responsibility, but I needed someone else to help me pray for the breakthrough. I had so many setbacks with my skin every time I tried this, so my mind would automatically focus on the fear of trying again and failing. Finally, I got mad and cried out for the mountain in my way to move! This is not what God meant for me, to have to go to ministry school like this. And it wasn't my idea of a good time, either.

One day a fellow student was in the car with me and she got a prophetic (a predictive) word from God for me. He said to her, "Tell Nancy to go shopping tonight for pants." What? Fear tried to settle in and steal that word. But I fought down that giant and I went for it. I drove at night in a torrential downpour of rain. I was fearful of driving in the dark because I couldn't see well at night. I clung to that steering wheel very tightly as my windshield wipers were flying back and forth! But I was determined to have the good things God had promised me, like new clothes. I had lived for many years without proper clothing or blankets. And God was totally giving me His strength. I felt His fearlessness and peace in the midst of my fear. So I kept going and when I got home with the pants, then I had to go through the ordeal of washing out the sizing in them many times, which was crazy. The next day I was intent on believing that I could wear those pants even though I had tried and failed so many times before. This was what the Bible called "taking authority." And I commanded my body to wear those pants.

The students noticed right away when I came in and cheered me on. So I absolutely would not let them be stolen from me again. It was painful to go through, but Jesus kept telling me those symptoms are not real. "Keep looking at Me, don't look at your skin," He said. And I watched as the skin rashes just melted away by believing Him. Wow! And God did it for me. He fought for me! And I stood firm on His promise.

We are three-part beings: spirit, soul, and body. And the good news is that the real *you* is a spirit. We *are* a spirit, we have a soul, and we live in a body. At salvation, our spirit becomes one with the Father. We become a temple for the Holy Spirit and we are not our own (1 Corinthians 6:17–20). We now have direct access to Him and the veil has been torn. Since our spirits are completely healed already on the cross, we must now take *authority* as a son or daughter of God and *command* that sickness to leave.

> So then, surrender to God (say "yes" to Him). Stand up to the devil and resist him (the sin, the lying symptoms, and the sickness) and he will turn and run away from you (examples added for the purpose of explanation).
>
> —James 4:7 (TPT)

If we can get our minds to agree with the truth in our spirits, it's two against one, and our bodies will follow along like little puppies. We are not meant to be victims of anything. We cannot let the enemy, our body, or our minds dominate us in any way. We are to take dominion on this earth. God says we are to be fruitful and to take dominion. . . (Genesis 1:28). And according to the definition of "dominion," this earth is our domain and we are to have the supreme authority and sovereignty over it. A world where *love* rules. We command the enemy to leave in the name of Jesus, and speak to our bodies and they are to follow what we say. Just like Jesus was able to command the storm to cease (Matthew 8:23–27), we have His same authority over the elements and our own bodies and minds. The definition of "authority" is: the power or right to give orders, make decisions, and enforce obedience. We are commanders who walk by faith in His Word, not by sight or by feelings.

We have been given a great and powerful positioning by God, above all principalities and powers. This is our privilege as His children. Inside of us is an omnipotent, omnipresent, and omniscient God (Hebrews 1:1–3). In every situation, we bring the "person" of Jesus and His supremacy. Woohoo! And He wants us to know it. To receive *revelation* and understanding of Him inside of us takes faith, but if we start praying this prayer we can begin to believe it:

> . . .that the God of our Lord Jesus Christ, the Father of glory, may give to you the spirit of wisdom and revelation in the knowledge of Him, the eyes of your understanding being enlightened; that you may know what is the hope of His calling, what are the riches of the glory of His inheritance in the saints, and what *is* the exceeding

greatness of His power toward us who believe, according to the working of His
mighty power which He worked in Christ
when He raised Him from the dead and
seated *Him* at His right hand in the heavenly *places,* far above all principality and
power and might and dominion, and every
name that is named, not only in this age
but also in that which is to come. And He
put all *things* under His feet, and gave Him
to be head over all *things* to the church,
which is His body, the fullness of Him who
fills all in all.

—Ephesians 1:17–23

The second prayer below also helps us understand what incredible authority He has given us.
He did not come into us with a little bit of power,
He came into us with it all. All the fullness of God
exists *inside* of us and He can do exceedingly far
above all we can ask or think according to that
resurrection power. This is not something we can
understand with our minds. This *revelation* needs
to be received by faith. So also pray this prayer:

For this reason I bow my knees to the Father of our Lord Jesus Christ, from whom
the whole family in heaven and earth is
named, that He would grant you, according
to the riches of His glory, to be strengthened
with might through His Spirit in the inner
man, that Christ may dwell in your hearts
through faith; that you, being rooted and
grounded in love, may be able to compre-

hend with all the saints what *is* the width
and length and depth and height—to know
the love of Christ which passes knowledge;
that you may be filled with all the fullness
of God. Now to Him who is able to do exceedingly abundantly above all that we ask
or think, according to the power that works
in us, to Him *be* glory in the church by
Christ Jesus to all generations, forever and
ever. Amen.

—Ephesians 3:14–21

I prayed these two prayers for three months
every day and my spiritual eyes were opened. I
started to have visions of Jesus while reading the
Bible. Christ has been seated far above all principalities and powers and all things are under His
feet. God gave Him to be head over all things to
the church, which is His body, (that is you and
me as saved children of God) the fullness of Him
who fills all in all. What this means is that all
things are under your feet too. We have to go over
and over this until we get it rooted down in our
hearts. Since He lives in us and we are His body,
we are far above every name and every sickness.
He was raised up and transferred all His authority
to us and made us sit together in the heavenly
places in Christ Jesus.

We should all be shouting at this point. This
is truly amazing! None of us will ever be able to
thank God enough for this incredibly royal position. We have a body on earth, but we are also
seated in heavenly places with Jesus at the right

hand of God and it's right now. We are citizens of heaven and citizens of earth. We have dual citizenship. He is the head and we are the body, and we are at the *power* of the center of the universe! We do not earn this position, or even learn it; we must *believe it.* It is ours by faith! And it is a powerful position. Literally we have His authority and power over every sickness, in our own body, as well as those we pray for. We don't need to beg God for the healing. He already did it. And because we have heard and trained ourselves in the miracle Words of God, we just reach out and take our healing by speaking to our bodies and to the mountain of circumstances. Tell the mountain what God says about it. It's His authority that has been delegated to us and He has charged us with enforcing it on the earth.

Paul tells us to put on the supernatural armor of God every day in Ephesians 6. So daily we dress ourselves. God would have me imagine putting on His armor every day. He told me I am like a sheriff here on earth enforcing the Word of God. And I would put on my boots, my belt of truth, my breastplate, my helmet, and take up my sword and my shield and continue to pray in the Spirit. Jesus came to destroy the works of the enemy and in His name so can we. We are to be forever grateful for our amazing Jesus!

God wants to turn us into powerful champions. He is a triumphant God and He is in love with us. He wants *us* powerful. He is *our* God! When you think about it, why wouldn't He want us totally filled with all of His power? We are His bride created to partner with Him on the earth and to fill it with His fullness. When we have totally committed our hearts to Him, He will flow right through us in power, in authority, and in love in order to heal and save not only us, but others too.

Take authority today and start doing what God says. Act, walk, and talk like God. Listen to and do what the Holy Spirit says. Sometimes He will tell us to pray, command, lay on hands, confess, act out things by faith, perform prophetic acts, fast and pray, or worship. It's all warfare. In the moment, God knows the best strategy. Don't focus on the problem, focus on the Promiser and His promise. We can imagine ourselves sitting at the throne with Him, holding onto our promise, and saying, "Yes Father," resisting the enemy and seeing the enemy flee from us in terror. It is not by our might, but by the Spirit. Most of our time should be spent adoring Jesus with our mind set on heaven, not on the problem. So be rejoicing, laughing, and having fun with God. God laughs at the enemy (Psalm 2:4). Sometimes God tickles me endlessly and has fun laughing with me and I get my breakthrough. We have the same power and authority that Jesus had when He walked on this earth when we are operating in the Spirit. And Jesus came to destroy the works of the enemy.

They said I had His authority at the Healing Room but I was really unaware of the seriousness of what God meant when He said to resist the enemy. And I got caught up in warfare a lot. And the enemy tried to mess me up big time. How could I command anything? Well, I needed to do it through Jesus, not of myself. I didn't get it right away, but I started saying it and commanding sickness to get out of my body. We are called to be aggressive with the enemy and bold as a lion. You cannot be passive! Jesus is from the tribe of the Lion of Judah and despite all the shame and torture of the cross, He did not give up. We were the joy set before Him. He did not lay down and submit to the enemy's plan to destroy our spirits, souls, and bodies. Jesus literally crushed the enemy and dragged him through the streets. And we should too.

We fight the good fight of faith by believing. The truth is we have it all! Everything God has is ours. He doesn't even call us to pray for the sick; He says just lay hands on them (Mark 16:17–18). We also have the authority and the power to lay hands on *ourselves* and release healing and move the enemy off by speaking to it.

> Behold, I give you the authority to trample on serpents and scorpions, and over all the power of the enemy, and nothing shall by any means hurt you.
> —Luke 10:19

Our authority rests on the Word and the power of God that is behind that authority. We can rejoice because all the power of heaven is backing us up.

Little children (believers, dear ones), you are
of God *and* you belong to Him and have [already] overcome them [the agents of the antichrist]; because He who is in you is
greater than he (satan) who is in the world
[of sinful mankind].

—1 John 4:4 (AMP)

The power that is in us is greater than that
which backs the enemy. And not only that, we
have the name of Jesus and a legal right to use
that name. We are already world overcomers!

Step 5

So it was critical for me to understand that I
could kick out the enemy. The only power he has
over you is the power you give him. My authority
is now the same as Jesus when I am operating in
the Spirit because I have submitted myself to Him
and it's not by my might, but by the Spirit. We
are the giants on this earth. We are like David
having spent time with our God in the secret
place, and knowing who our God is, easily take
out any enemy giant that stands before us. And
exactly like Jesus said, we will do the greater
works, even greater than Him, because He is forever interceding for us.

Prayer for activation of His Kingdom authority: Father, I want to do the greater works so
I ask you to activate the Christ within me and all
of His Omnipotent power and authority. Give me
a Spirit of wisdom and revelation in the knowledge
of you and give me a Spirit of might that grounds

me in your love. Show me that I have all the fullness of God inside me and where I am seated in the heavenlies far above every principality, power, might, and dominion. Teach me about putting on your armor daily as I go out, compelled by love, to release Your goodness. Teach me the authority of a son or daughter of God and how to command and release the resurrection healing power inside of me. I declare this healing power is released in my own body now so that I may go about doing good and healing all others who are oppressed. Thank you. In the name of Jesus, amen.

Chapter 6

The Dynamite Power of the Holy Spirit

*But truly I am full of power by the Spirit of
the LORD, and of justice and might. . .*
—Micah 3:8

I WAS ABOUT to find out what a sudden move
of God was really like. God was going to radically
change me and propel me ahead at full speed.
Why? Because I refused to give up. I wanted
more of Him at any cost, and more healing. And
I got it. They told me at the Healing Rooms that I
needed the power of a baptism in the Holy Spirit.
That is where the real power comes in for healing.
What? I thought I had asked Jesus into my heart,
"You mean there is more?" I said. "Yes." The more
is the Holy Spirit; pure explosive, *dunamis* power
that transforms you, and not only that, He is absolute, pure love. My heart soared with the
thought of it.

69

After the disciples had prayed in the upper room, waiting for the power, the Holy Spirit came like the sound of a mighty rushing wind and filled the whole house. Fire sat upon them and they were all filled with the Holy Spirit and began speaking in other languages and tongues (Acts 2). So what they got was a way of praying, called "tongues," that was from God. It was also called the tongues of angels, and it was the Holy Spirit now praying through them for God's perfect will.

So I wanted it too because God is the same yesterday, today, and forever (Hebrews 13:8). I thought about it, back and forth, yes or no, but my heart would not give up. I received the baptism as they prayed for me at the Healing Rooms, but I didn't get this prayer language called tongues. I called prayer lines also and had them pray but I couldn't seem to pray out in a tongue like they described. I got Joyce Meyer's book, called *Knowing God Intimately* that talked about going to deeper and deeper levels of intimacy and knowing God. Well, I was desperately hungry to be healed and to know all the levels of God too. So I read about receiving the baptism of the Holy Spirit in her book and prayed for it by myself, just the book, me, and God. And sure enough I started speaking in tongues, exactly like it said. I wanted to see how it was happening so I ran to the mirror and watched myself speaking. What an amazing discovery! How did this work?

I only prayed for five minutes and went off to bed that night. But there was a battle going on because I could feel an anger all around me. What was I so mad about? Wow! I tried to get rid of the feeling. Strange, I thought. Then in the morning I woke up. I was sure I should probably never pray that way again because it had stirred up so much anger. If I was anything, it was fearful, not angry. So who was angry? Well, it became clear in a minute; it was the enemy. Satan knows that with the power of the Holy Spirit within us and upon us, he doesn't stand a chance!

I went to do my exercises. My doctor had told me to do any exercise I could every day to keep my circulation going. My feet were so swollen I couldn't get shoes on at all, so I had to wear sandals that I left unbuckled. It was embarrassing and uncomfortable. But people pretended not to notice. Even the podiatrist said if I couldn't get an abscess to heal on my foot, they were going to have to cut my foot off! Another horrible lie. So all I could do at the time was to lay on my back and do calisthenics like bicycle exercises.

It was at this point that I saw my feet above me. I had to look at them again. They were totally different. All the swelling had gone out of them overnight. They had bones again that I could see. Normal size! I shot off the couch and looked again. No one prayed for me. I did nothing but get my prayer language and the baptism in the Holy Spirit. No wonder *something* was angry! It was the enemy, trying to stop me from having the gift of the Holy Spirit and His miraculous prayer language. It changed my life forever. Shoes were a possibility again even after years of wearing sandals in cold and very wet weather. It was a great and sudden miracle that absolutely proved to me the power of tongues. Yay God! I was so utterly grateful. And the Holy Spirit has been my best friend ever since.

Before Jesus left this earth, He comforted His disciples by telling them He would send to them the Promise of the Father. And they would be able to carry on without Him and they would even be able to do greater works than He did on the earth (John 14:12). He was going to send them out to raise the dead, heal the sick, and cleanse the lepers without Him. And it would be by this Promise of the Father. That promise is the Holy Spirit.

When Jesus got baptized by John the Baptist, the heavens opened up and a dove descended and rested upon Jesus, and the voice of the Father was heard to say, "This is my beloved Son, in whom I am well pleased" (Matthew 3:16–17). Jesus came to earth and gave up His divine right as God to be born into a body in order to fulfill all the law so we could be forgiven by God. So when Jesus, who had lived a life without sin, was baptized, He was totally filled with God the Holy Spirit, and went about doing good and healing all who were oppressed. Fast-forward to today; Jesus is now ascended to heaven, but God the Holy Spirit is still here on earth.

But John made it clear by telling them, "There is one coming who is mightier than I. He is supreme. In fact, I'm not worthy of even being his slave. I can only baptize you in this river, but he will baptize you into the Spirit of holiness and into his raging fire."

—Luke 3:16

This is what the disciples were told to wait for after Jesus ascended. He said to wait for the Promise of the Father; wait and you will be filled with power. What is that power? It's called *dunamis* power which means, in the Greek, "force, specifically miraculous power (usually by implication a miracle itself), ability, abundance, meaning, might, miracle power, strength, violence, mighty (wonderful) work." Woohoo! That is the Holy Spirit! One lightning bolt from the Holy Spirit is like having one billion volts of electric love flood through you. He is a mighty power of miracle-working ability! Straight-up power and fire! All for the good of healing God's people and the earth and bringing resurrection life back to them, to God be the glory. He is part of the Godhead and is on earth today.

> Behold, I send the Promise of My Father upon you; but tarry in the city of Jerusalem until you are endued with power from on high.
>
> —Luke 24:49

Do whatever you have to do to get the baptism in the Holy Spirit and your prayer language. Praying in tongues is the most powerful, most miraculous gift ever from God. The enemy fought me on this, tried to cause me to doubt, to stop, and to put fake symptoms on me that would come and go. He even went to the point of attacking me every time I tried to pray in this manner. But do not settle for his lies. Take down those giants and keep after it. I learned to pray it out in the car, and to set a timer to train myself to pray for longer. I even learned to pray it while reading my Bible, under my breath when I was around other people, or inside myself when I was eating or talking. It is the answer to the verse "pray without ceasing" (1 Thessalonians 5:17). You can literally do it anywhere at any time. Do it! It really works. I decided then that no power in hell was going to stop me from getting all that Jesus had for me, including this miraculous gift of tongues.

According to Dr. Bill Hamon, what you are doing when you open your mouth is you are letting open the gates of a huge dynamo power-plant called Holy Spirit. He generates electricity like a wheel within a wheel and delivers the power of God, the presence of God, the love of God, and the anointing of God, etc.

Here is what happens when you desire and ask for the Baptism of the Holy Spirit:

> And when Paul laid his hands on each of the twelve, the Holy Spirit manifested and they immediately spoke in tongues and prophesied.
>
> —Acts 19:6

And when you get your tongue/prayer language, there are benefits that praying in your natural language do not have: it builds you up in *holy*

74

faith, fastens your heart to the love of God and His mercy, gives compassion to others, and snatches others out of the fire to save them.

> But you, *my* delightfully loved friends, constantly and progressively build yourselves up on the foundation of your most holy faith by praying every moment in the Spirit. Fasten your hearts to the love of God and receive the mercy of our Lord Jesus Christ, who gives us eternal life. Keep being compassionate to those who still have doubts, and snatch others out of the fire to save them. Be merciful over and over to them, but always couple your mercy with the fear of God. Be extremely careful to keep yourselves free from the pollutions of the flesh.
> —Jude 1:20–23 (TPT)

And when we don't know how to pray for something, the Holy Spirit will pray through us God's perfect will, even though we may not understand it.

> And in a similar way, the Holy Spirit takes hold of us in our human frailty to empower us in our weakness. For example, at times we don't even know how to pray, or know the best things to ask for. But the Holy Spirit rises up within us to super-intercede on our behalf, pleading to God with emotional sighs too deep for words. God, the searcher of the heart, knows fully our longings, yet he also understands the desires of

the Spirit, because the Holy Spirit passionately pleads before God for us, his holy
ones, in perfect harmony with God's plan
and our destiny.

—Romans 8:26–27 (TPT)

The voice of God cries out in tongues through
your spirit and He sometimes goes so deeply and
so powerfully you may be lost in passionate sobs
or the highest ecstatic joys. Even though you may
not understand it, let Him pray it out for you. It's
the effective, fervent prayer of the righteous that
avails much (James 5:16). Things you didn't
know before start to bubble up in your mind. God
starts to give wisdom and strategies from heaven
for your life. It is His language, and since you are
born again of the Spirit, this is the language we
should be speaking as the new creation. And
praying it unceasingly. He can release whatever
you need through praying it: purification, healing,
deliverance, wisdom, direction, words of knowledge, joyous laughter, visions, breakthrough, refreshing, inspired thought, etc. Nothing is
impossible for God.

One time the Holy Spirit challenged me to pray
for an hour in tongues. "Okay," I said. I happened to be out driving and thought I should find
a place outside to walk and pray. So I pulled into
a strip mall and found a sidewalk next to a
wooded area, where there were no people. And I
prayed out loud in my prayer language and really
went after it. I didn't know at the time *what* the
Holy Spirit was praying. It was a mystery to me

but it was passionate in the Spirit and I had fun with the Lord. I drove off that day feeling good about it.

Two years later God asked me to go locate the new low-income housing development that had just been completed and take a tour. Now as an outreach pastor, I had it on my heart to help the homeless and was out many times passing out bags of food and talking with them about their plight. So I was excited to see this place. I had been praying regularly for low-income housing in unity with our local churches and pastors. I got the address and located it on my map. I drove out there for a tour. And guess where it was? It was at the wooded area where I had prayed that day in tongues. All the trees had been torn down and low-income apartments, plus some units for the homeless, had sprung up there. I was totally awestruck. I knew for sure God had used my prayer in tongues that day to somehow prepare the way for this gift of low-income housing. How cool was that? God works in mysterious ways and He never told me anything about it. Wow Jesus! It's the miraculous language of heaven. Our "Father tongue."

There was another time when God would ask me to drive over to a particular neighborhood to pray. He did not tell me the reason, I just followed Him. I would drive by it and for two years He would have me go in, park, and pray in tongues around the neighborhood. And go on my way. I blessed everyone and prayed. I loved His adventures! Yet when we were forced to move out of our rental in 30 days, we had no idea how we could find a place that fast. My husband started searching, and it had always been hard to find a place because of my strict allergy requirements. But God!

My husband contacted a realtor to help us. Just that morning, a homeowner had come in and listed a property. So I went along with my husband and the realtor to see three properties we might rent. We saw some interesting homes, but for the last one the realtor turns onto this road where I had been praying for two years. And my mouth dropped open and my whole being was gripped in *awe.* I said in my head, "No way, no way! Really? This street?" And the house we looked at was beautiful and perfect, and even met all my strict requirements and had everything on both my husband's and my dream lists. It was a miracle house. Three years later we bought it. And Jesus knew the whole time! He must have loved the look on my face and the fun of surprising His daughter. God is so fun!

God can work miracles and mysteries through your prayer language. Make it your daily goal to pray in tongues. In the New Testament, Paul even said he prayed in tongues more than *all* of the Corinthians. If you want to walk in signs and wonders, get your prayer language today.

When someone speaks in tongues, no one understands a word he says, because he's not speaking to people, but to God—he is speaking intimate mysteries in the Spirit. . . The one who speaks in tongues advances his own spiritual progress.

—1 Corinthians 14:2,4

Step 6

The most miraculous gift of all is having the Holy Spirit poured out over your heart continuously. This is what Jesus came to give me, a baptism of His *fire and passionate love*. And now that I know, I would never want to do this without my glorious friend the Holy Spirit. His is the *power* you need to fulfill every miraculous promise. I am forever His student and I pray that you will know He is absolutely loyal and faithful. In praying the Holy Spirit's language, you will find He weeps for His children, He is profoundly wise, and He is infinitely deep. And you will find the Holy Spirit to be endlessly peaceful and comforting, and the most patient teacher you have ever known.

Prayer for baptism in the Holy Spirit: Holy Spirit, you are the Promise of the Father and I desire to have you as my most tender friend and God. Jesus, baptize me and fill me with the Holy Spirit and with fire and power from on high. Continuously pour out the love of the Holy Spirit into my positioned heart. All glory be to God. By my free will and by faith I choose to speak in tongues and receive my power-packed, demon-busting prayer language from heaven. Holy Spirit, it is a gift to me from you and I desire to have it. I open my mouth and you will fill it with your new language. I let it flow. Thank you. In the name of Jesus, amen.

Chapter 7

Engaging the Lord of the Breakthrough in Worship

His head and his hair were white like wool—
white as glistening snow. And his eyes were like
flames of fire! His feet were gleaming like bright
metal, as though they were glowing in a fire, and
his voice was like the roar of many rushing
waters. In his right hand he held seven stars,
and out of his mouth was a sharp, double-edged
sword. And his face was shining like the
brightness of the blinding sun!
—Revelation 1:14–16 (TPT)

GODS WANTS US hot after His glorious Presence, His voice, His Love, and His Word. It says in the Song of Solomon 1:3 ". . .for your lovely name is 'Flowing Oil.' No wonder the brides-to-be adore you." Jesus is our magnificently thrilling and delightful friend. He wants to be known and experienced. And no power on earth can stop us from His heart. He calls us to come up into glory in the book of Revelation and we have free access. He wants us as jealous for Him as He is for us. He wants a bride who will not compromise, without spot or wrinkle, not double-minded, but single-eyed, wanting nothing of this world, but to behold Him.

Since we become what we behold, He tells us to let go of everything and to look at Him. Make it your intention to see Him. Pray and ask for a Spirit of Wisdom and Revelation to open the eyes of your heart so you can see Him before you as you worship, and you will start to have visions of Him (see Ephesians 1:17–18). If you can envision even a little bit of Him, you will begin to get closer and closer to His heart and your eyes will open more. We need to draw near to Him and behold the beauty of His holiness. Come on! We must be hungrier than ever in these times.

He wants us to sing to Him a love song in worship. He is the divine romance. He wants to give Himself to us like a never-ending waterfall of love. He is always seeking out His beloved but He loves to be sought out too. We actually can't get enough of Him and the more you receive of Jesus, the more you burn and hunger for more. And Jesus will fill the hungry. Blessed are those who hunger and thirst for righteousness, for they will be filled (Matthew 5:6). Even more than that, be curious enough to ask Him to explain things to you and He will. To hear His voice is most precious indeed.

I joined Destiny International School of Ministry seven months into my healing and the theme of the school was to begin each day with worship. So during those three years, four mornings a week, we started with worship. I learned that God deserves our best in the morning and I fell in love with Jesus in worship. I would walk through the sanctuary praising God with all my heart and I would feel him all around me and my heart would pound with excitement. Supernatural things would start to happen and I would be lifted out of the battle happening in my mind. I would break through into freedom and joy because the Bible says where the Spirit of the Lord is there is freedom (2 Corinthians 3:17).

A grateful open heart is also huge to anyone who needs to be healed. If we start being thankful for the health we have, the family we have, the life we have been given, we will see immediately that the complaining heart we just had starts to melt. When we are thankful, our heart starts to open a tiny bit. When that happens we realize, oh, so many others have it much worse than we do. Also, it is a principle in the Kingdom, that when we start to think about good things, we will become those things. Gratitude is how we enter into God. Enter his gates with thanksgiving (Psalm 100:4). Thankfulness totally opens us up like throwing open the windows on a hot day; the Holy Spirit will rush in like a cool breeze. So throw open your gates and let joy, love, and peace rush in. He is joy itself!

I have been caught up in the Spirit of God many times and taken up to experience the throne room in worship and you can too. God wants us to come before His throne. This is where the authority of heaven rules over our circumstances and where we have come to Mt. Zion. He calls us to come up and to ascend in worship, to be carried away in the Spirit (Revelation 4:1). God does not want us *under* our circumstances, He wants us *over* them. So come up above. There is healing in the glory as we let go of all our struggles and take hold of Jesus. In that place with Jesus, you forget who you are, and it's only Him. I would get lost in Him and forget all about that my body was crying: "What about me? What about me? What about me?" In that absolute passion to have more of Him and less of me, I found myself, beautifully filled with Him. John 15:4 (ABPE) says: "Stay with Me, and I am in you. . ." When you get to Him, lock into Him, stay with Him. Worship with all your heart. He is worthy!

Jesus is joy! Incredible ecstatic joy. If you get into worshipping with all your heart, you will soon find out about His joy. And His laughter. In His joy you are strengthened. Because "the joy of the Lord is our strength" (Nehemiah 8:10). And when you start to laugh, that "merry heart is good like medicine" (Proverbs 17:22). So let yourself be full of joy and laughter. Have fun with Jesus. It is part of God's healing. And who would think to use that strategy? Only God! His healing medicine is joy and laughter. As you worship, you

can't help but to feel His joyful heart, so let it bubble out of you in strength. A good belly laugh is
so good for us. We can laugh during worship with
Jesus, it's okay to be free. At home Jesus and I
laugh all the time in worship. . . because He is
showing me funny pictures of sliding down water
slides into the Holy Spirit river of life, and flying
through heaven like an eagle. And we have fun
running and laughing around the house because
His favorite game is to play hide-and-seek. So be
childlike and let Him bring you into His joy. There
is nothing like oneness with our King Jesus!

God will lavishly enthrone our hearts with
Himself and cause all our enemies to scatter in
his supreme sovereignty. To enthrone means to
install a monarch on a throne. And in Psalm 22:3
it says, "But You are holy, enthroned in the
praises of Israel." In our praises, the enemy's plan
gets overthrown by His omnipotence. So sing to
Him. Praise Him. We are also creating an atmosphere on earth when we are near the throne room
of God, and no enemy can come near. We are
worshipping in heaven in the glory realm and *He
changes us* as we gaze upon Him. One Sunday as
I was praying for more authority for breakthrough, God said to me, "If you want more authority, Nancy, then get right next to my heart."
Woohoo, that's exactly where we need to be! All-
out love for our Jesus. He is the Almighty powerful God!

As our hearts fling wide open, God loves to battle for us in worship! It says in 2 Chronicles 20:22

"At the very moment they began to sing and give praise, the Lord caused the armies of Ammon, Moab, and Mount Seir to start fighting among themselves." He set ambushes and routed them out as they sang. It is thrilling to my heart to have Jesus fight for me and crush my enemies. I love to go for it like King David, unashamed in expressive worship. When Paul and Silas were in jail praying and singing hymns to God ". . .suddenly a massive earthquake came. . . doors flew open and the chains of every prisoner fell off" (Acts 16:25–26). Wow!

One time I was in church worshipping and singing and the praise song called *Running* by Hillsong came on. So I heard the Lord say to me very clearly "Run." Well, I hadn't run for years because every time I tried, I got intense pain in my knees and would have setbacks and pain for weeks. But, I obeyed and ran a little ways. Amazingly, it didn't hurt, so I went a quarter way around the church, then that word kept repeating in my heart, "Run," so I ran in faith all the way around and there was no pain. So I went a second lap around, no pain. Then a third lap around, and I was totally healed. And I have been healed ever since. It was an instantaneous miracle. And all I did was obey in the middle of a worship service. My actions cooperated with my faith because by works my faith is made perfect (James 2:14–22). God was fighting for me in that instant as I risked it all to step out in faith. And thanks to Jesus, He can do it for all of us. Just ask Him to do it again or anything you need healing for, and believe Him.

Many, many get healed in the worship services here in America and all over the world. It is a matter of your hunger and expectation as you enter into the miraculous. He loves to show off! Whenever you feel the presence of the Lord around you, miracles are possible. He is very present and tangible in the worship times, and sometimes comes in a glory cloud full of miracles. Stretch out and ask Him. Expect Him to come. What are we expecting of our God? Be careful not to dismiss the little ideas that come into your mind—the still, small voice that says, "Try it." Pay attention. Many times we miss it. But if we are alert, and watching for Him, we can *tap* into what He is doing. It is sometimes a whisper, or a picture, or a dream, or just a knowing. If we are sure it's Him, our faith will rise up and we go with it and participate in our miracle. We are called to live by faith and not by sight.

In worship, God loves us to be absolutely free, free, free! There are many Hebrew words that describe how to worship God. From lifting hands, to bowing, to kneeling, to singing, to shouting, to clapping, to playing instruments, to dancing etc. He says seek Me with your whole heart, and you will find Me (Jeremiah 29:13). This means we have to surrender and put down all our cares at the cross, roll them on Him, and open up our hands. To worship is to delight in Him. We delight ourselves in Him, let go of all our worries, look up, and open up our hearts to bless Him and to receive whatever He wants to give (Psalm 37:4–5). And believe me, He is ready to encounter you! We come into the kingdom as a child, thanking him, and believing in Him. Ask God to give you an encounter at the throne. Prophesy and declare over yourself that you are going to the throne room and set your face like a flint to have it. And be thankful.

Also keep your home filled with the atmosphere of worship. I have literally told this to hundreds of people through the years. It works. It purifies and cleanses our homes and chases out the enemy. I have worship music going in my home all through the day and night because I want my home to be a house of worship. You are making a statement before all of heaven that God deserves to be worshipped and that your desire is for Him. Several times I have found golden glory dust around my speakers and I know it is from the worship. God and the angels love it. You are creating an open heaven and literally a ladder from heaven to earth where the angels ascend and descend (Genesis 28:12).

Step 7

I discovered that falling in love with and engaging Jesus in worship is everything! He is all we need, He is the one Who has everything and completes us in every way. We actually want the Healer, the One who is our total healing: spirit, soul, and body. Coming to Him in worship will enthrone Him on your heart, thanksgiving will open all your gates, and He will battle and show off for you in worship. In all of heaven this is what they are doing forever: Crying Holy, Holy, Holy. And our wildly loving and powerful King wants us to come up and be right there with Him in the throne room where there is no sickness. In paradise!

Prayer for a thankful heart of worship: Father, turn my heart into one of thanksgiving and gratitude. I want to be grateful for everything and see everything through thankful eyes. Give me a hunger and a spirit to worship you with all my might and all my heart. Take me up in the Spirit to the glorious atmosphere of heaven to encounter you in all your Glory. If I can see it in the Spirit during worship, I can declare it on earth and receive it. I want heaven on earth. Give me fresh faith to believe again. Show me how to expect miracles in your Presence during worship. Pour out your Spirit on me again and lead me into your laughter and joy. Help me tap into your still, small voice; I want to participate in my miracle. Thank you. In the name of Jesus, amen.

Chapter 8

Healing Rooms and Ministers

Are there any sick among you? Then ask the elders of the church to come and pray over the sick and anoint them with oil in the name of our Lord. And the prayer of faith will heal the sick and the Lord will raise them up, and if they have committed sins they will be forgiven.
—James 5:14–15 (TPT)

"YOU CAN DO IT! Come on!" Jesus said. He kept whispering to me I should get to a Healing Room near me. They have some real prayer warriors there who know their authority as sons of God. And I felt Him literally cause me to trust Him as we went every Saturday off Camano Island in 2010 to the Healing Room for prayer. My husband would make me a bed in the back of our Jeep because at that point I had so much swelling in my legs and pain I could not sit down. And we would drive off with me hoping and praying for a miracle, while trying to push out thoughts of doubt.

There was a Healing Room about an hour's drive from us and I would have such setbacks from the ride and such a battle that I only went three times and really wanted to give up. A few times I had felt His power but I needed to keep going even though it was so far away! So I prayed with all my heart for one to open up closer. And I made a few calls to the main office. Then about three weeks later Jesus guided me to check one more time on the Healing Room website to see if anything came up. And I found the announcement for a new Healing Room closer to my home that was opening at 9:00AM the next morning. Oh my gosh! God had answered my prayer! And Jesus proved He loved me so much over and over. So it was their opening day, and my husband and I showed up with me lying in the back of the truck and he brought me in through that door right at 9:00AM. We were the first ones to walk through the door the day it opened in our area.

They had created an atmosphere of safety and I felt that I could be open and honest. They explained that the illness was really an attack from satan and that God wanted me well. Someone was trying to kill me and it wasn't Jesus; it was satan. So I got righteously angry and started fighting back for my life. I was mad! I hated what the enemy had done to me and my family. I felt like destroying every form of sickness on the planet and I still do! I was not going to lie down and take it anymore.

God opened the door so I kept asking my husband to take me. My mind was set on not wanting to be a burden since I couldn't drive there myself. I felt really guilty. But Jesus wouldn't let me be that way. He said: "Ask him." So I did, and my husband took me and I went by faith with my heart full of hope and expectation that something would break through for me. I rode lying down in the back of the Jeep for the 25-minute drive. I felt really embarrassed about it at first, but I was determined. I could see the effects of the prayer right away. I was releasing forgiveness to others and myself, and God was closing every door to the enemy.

We first got introduced to the Healing Rooms when we moved to Spokane, WA in 2001 because my mother-in-law's Lutheran pastor had received a miracle there. She and her husband had been praying for a baby for years without success. Shortly after going to the Healing Rooms for prayer, she got pregnant, thanks to Jesus. And she was telling everyone her testimony. She picked me up to go there, and told me all about this place where they pray for others. She said it was a place where the Christians believed the Bible literally and that Jesus is still healing today. So, I went, and I was going to ask God to do a miracle for me too. I was filled with this incredible peace while waiting there. More peace than I had ever felt. My whole body went deeply peaceful and they hadn't even prayed for me yet. I told the pastor what I was feeling, and she sensed that God was preparing my heart. The team prayed and I remember that I got a little better and was encouraged to read the Bible. I remember them telling me the best thing to read in the Bible would be the books Matthew, Mark, Luke, and John. But I didn't do it. And we never did find a church in Spokane to join.

The Healing Rooms can be a great transitional place to get healed if you have not been to church or are currently not going to one. They are a ministry whose goal is to help all people, but especially those who are not in a church yet or whose churches do not yet have the revelation that Jesus heals today.

I am in a church now that believes in healing, but I wasn't then, and I was so grateful for the Healing Rooms. They just pray and don't put pressure on you one way or the other. They don't counsel; they are trained to minister to you under the guidance and direction of the Holy Spirit. The point is that I didn't know how to get healed on my own; I had to get with some trained prayer warriors who knew their authority and how to use their faith. We may not have built up our faith enough yet to believe God for a miracle. But if we are in a crisis, God has trained ministers that can help us with our needs.

I went back for prayer to healing ministers over and over again until I got my healing. One prayer team member told me: "If you don't get your healing right away, don't give up, keep coming to God until you get it. He has promised you." So I did. And when my healing wasn't manifesting yet, that word would burn in my heart. . . He has promised you. So I kept humbly coming. I couldn't do it on my own. The good news is that there is help! And we can rely on trained intercessors and rely on their faith until we get our own.

They taught me to be tough and to refuse to allow the enemy to have any power over me spiritually. The people there were great prayer warriors that commanded the enemy to get off my life and to stop torturing me with fear and physical symptoms. By sticking with it and going four Saturdays in a row, I was healed enough to sit up and drive myself over for prayer. I was celebrating! I was also calling during the week for prayer down in Colorado to Andrew Wommack Ministries because they have a fantastic prayer line. And Jesus stood up for me! He would get me up on Saturday mornings and tell me with enthusiasm: "Come on, you can do it!" and we would go for more prayer. And I tried to smile at Jesus and have a good attitude, but sometimes I felt like giving up and I really had to make myself go.

You can also search for pastors or evangelists that have a healing ministry near you because God is moving in fantastic ways across America today and in healing meetings all over the country. We can get healed by live stream over the internet, through TV, live Facebook, CD, DVD, podcast, etc. If we can believe, all things are possible to us according to our faith (Mark 9:23). And because God is everywhere present, we don't necessarily have to go there. Someone that can believe on the Presence of God that has radical faith for a healing, can even get healed alone with just the Bible and the Word of God. But if we are struggling with our faith and need to tap into someone else's faith, there are many options.

God is showing up in testimony after testimony around the country. Some of the places that I plugged into and watched or traveled to are the Healing Rooms which are across the nation and worldwide, Bethel Church in Redding, California, and Andrew Wommack's ministry in Colorado, which is also worldwide. Andrew Wommack has a website with many teachings for free. Start listening to or reading about their teachings on healing. Stay with it, hunger for it, and God will always fill the hungry. We must get a boldness and an aggressiveness to go for it and ask for our own healing. Get to the altar at church and ask. I even recently learned that the Catholic Church near me has a healing prayer chain before service where people come to get healing prayer. Ask for a Pastor who may have a revelation of healing in your area.

If you don't have a church, get on line and find the nearest Healing Room in your area. Currently Bethel Church has a healing conference once a year and when we were there the first night over 400 people got healed! God was moving sovereignly across the whole building. It was totally miraculous! Let the Holy Spirit lead—He lives inside you—and refuse to fear or to let doubt or religious beliefs and theology stop you. Where the Spirit of the Lord is, there is total freedom. God wants to give you the gift of your miracle; His answer is yes. So renounce anything in your heart that says He is not that good. He *is* that good. God is telling us He wants to show Himself strong for us.

Also, watching healing testimonies is a great thing to do to build our faith. They are powerful because they create an atmosphere for miracles and give us the courage to ask God to do a miracle for us too. They build our faith. If He did a miracle for them, why wouldn't He do one for you too? I watched healing testimonies over and over again. Why? Because I was gleaning techniques for breakthrough. Basically, what we are doing is getting others' revelation of healing and making it our own. So please take my testimony, and ask Jesus to do it again for you. And God is no respecter of persons; He will do it for all of us.

God is even doing such fantastic healings now in some places, that they no longer even have to pray or lay on hands, He is just moving through the crowds in the anointed atmosphere of worship, glory, faith, and relationship. It takes our hunger and desperation to pull on the healing anointing and the glory. It also comes through a childlike faith that doesn't have it all reasoned out (Mark 10:13–16). It is just God. Miracles, signs, and wonders follow Him. We can't figure them out, nor do we need to. The fact is, God is eager to heal us and miracles are easy for Him. They take no effort at all for Him. Whatever you pray, believe you receive, then you will have whatsoever you pray. And healing lines up with Scripture, so we have God's Word on it. Healing is taught throughout the Bible. It is God's very nature.

Step 8

This next step then is critical if you are new to the faith. Get up, step out on the water and go to a Healing Room and/or an anointed Church whose pastor believes that God is doing miraculous healings today. Don't wait another minute! God responds to our faith (Matthew 9:29). You are worth the effort. You are most precious to God and to me. Don't bow for another minute to the enemy's lies; cry out to God! I had to let all my pride go; I realized that I didn't really know what to do anymore. In that place of neediness, God will pour out His grace!

Prayer for direction to a Healing Minister: Father, I hunger and thirst for you and for your promise of healing and wholeness. I ask that you would give me clear wisdom and revelation on whom you would like me to align with for my healing. I need you, God! I need a place that operates in real faith! Lead me to an anointed healing ministry that is under proper covering and that operates in incredible faith and miracles. Teach me, Lord, there is nothing impossible for you and how to receive my healing. We are so thankful that you have all the solutions! We love all you do for us and want you to get all the glory. In the name of Jesus, amen.

Chapter 9

Resting in the Love of the Father

But those who wait for the Lord (who expect, look for, and hope in Him) will gain new strength and renew their power, they will lift up their wings (and rise up close to God) like eagles (rising toward the sun); they will run and not become weary, they will walk and not grow tired.
—Isaiah 40:31 (AMP)

A REALLY FANTASTIC thing happened to me! I discovered that God is so big He could heal me when I rested in His Presence without a prayer minister or even being at church. And He wants to do that for you too. It's called *grace* and it is always available—it's His unmerited favor and blessing. We are saved by grace through faith. And it is our Father's good pleasure to give to us the Kingdom and what we need (Luke 12:32). God is gracious and He is the one who bestows good-will and lovingkindness. He is the greater one who bestows gifts on the lesser. He always wants to increase us in love, pleasure, joy, and freedom; no strings attached. So this is a place where you position yourself to wait on the Lord. Become the believer who is a *receiver*. He wants us to expect, look for, and hope in Him and His promises in the Word, and He also wants to give us an encounter with the One who wrote it. So get ready and rise on up your wings and get close to God; He wants to encounter you in rest and He will come with His lavishing love and gifts.

This is a place for us to *trust*. We can't earn it or learn it; we must believe it by faith. In this case, we lay everything down. I mean *everything*. And we wait for Him and we allow Him to move and heal what He knows is best. We turn off all the trying and all the efforts to get healed and come to Him. Zechariah 4:6 says: "Not by might nor by power, but by my Spirit, says the Lord Almighty." We keep surrendering it all to the Lord. Every circumstance: just lay it down, casting all your cares and worries upon Him and trust in His faithfulness and let your spirit soar.

This is a practice of becoming still and knowing that He is God. There is a place in His perfect peace where we can immediately relax. It's called "entering His rest" (Hebrews 4:9–11). Like when you finally sit down and your body relaxes, there is a similar reaction for your soul and spirit. Your mindset immediately changes into a sense of peacefulness as you let go and let God. The Prince of Peace is inside of you. Even God rested on the 7th day and He blesses rest. And He has made us to sit at the throne. It's a throne attitude. We are seated and resting in His love.

Others call it "soaking" or "soaking prayer." In most Healing Rooms, they have a soaking room to come into where there is soft, anointed worship music playing. You can come and rest in the rich and peaceful atmosphere of His grace and prepare your heart to receive before coming into a prayer room. There now are many soaking groups going on at different churches. But you can create your own also, or soak by yourself in worship. I like to imagine I am soaking in the glory light of Christ.

> He offers a resting place for me in his luxurious love. His tracks take me to an oasis of peace, the quiet brook of bliss. That's where he restores and revives my life. He opens before me pathways to God's pleasure and leads me along in his footsteps of righteousness so that I can bring honor to his name.
>
> —Psalm 23:2–3 (TPT)

It is really God's love that heals us. We only need to give Him a chance. Most of us are praying and having a one-way monologue, but do we really allow God to *love* us, hold us, or talk to us? Are we willing to listen and not rush for a moment or two? In this type of healing prayer, we don't ask for anything and we don't intercede, we just climb up on His lap and rest in His peace, or sink down into His river of Life (Ezekiel 47), expecting Him to heal whatever He wants to heal in us as His children. Our God is omnipresent and because it is God's nature to heal us, we can receive anytime or anywhere by faith. We allow God to bestow His love on us for a change. He loves us right where we are. He made us and He loves us unconditionally just the way we are, mistakes and all. And just like there is joy every morning, there is healing every time we come before Him. He *is* healing.

So put on some soaking music (from healing ministries like Julie True or Grace Williams), and sit or lay down and allow yourself to imagine a waterfall washing down over you. It's God's love and it never stops because the Spirit is given without measure (John 3:34). It's like pure, crystal-clear, warm glory water from the throne of God (Revelation 22:1–5). It fills us with His love. He wants to soak us like a sponge in love. He wants to wash over us with waterfalls of love and heal our hearts. God is love. If your mind wanders, keep bringing it back to the thought that "God is love." If you can visualize the face of Jesus, that is even better. We are to look away from the natural realm and fasten our gaze upon the loving face of Jesus. Be open to God. And let Him fill you. Over and over He wants to wrap us in blankets of love.

Sometimes people will strive and perform for years for God like Martha, Mary's sister, but all they really needed was one minute in His perfect anointing, and they would have been changed forever. They needed a God encounter. God is eager to help us! His love heals us and when we rest, we are just receiving. There is a well of living waters inside us (John 4:1–15). And Jesus wants to give us a drink so we will never thirst again. And the water that He gives us will become within us a fountain of water springing up into everlasting life.

One time when I was talking to my pastor, I said, "Well I have tried this and I have tried that." And He said, "That's exactly the problem, you are trying." Let God do it for you. Let God lead you. For most of us, the hardest thing God asks us to do is to release all our cares, stress, and worries. And it's in that surrender, that we finally learn to *trust*. We are called to rest and to trust in a God for whom there is nothing impossible.

They would pray for me, "Nancy, if you don't sit down and rest, God will." That was a good word right there! He literally wants to work for you. It's one of the most common problems we see in the Healing Rooms. We carry all these burdens. And many times people will have shoulder pain because of it. But Jesus needs us to rest, relax, and surrender so that we carry no burdens and no fears. If you have shoulder pain right now because you have been carrying your problems, just surrender them to Jesus and receive your healing. He is always right now. He says that we are to carry no troubles at all! In order to help us with this, He gives us one of the most incredible promises in the Bible:

> Pour out all your worries and stress upon Him and leave them there, for He always tenderly cares for you.
> —1 Peter 5:7 (TPT)

As we rest with Him and get quiet, we will begin to feel the tangible Presence of God and He will start to talk to us and show us the wisdom we need. In the stillness, you can start to sense a flow of His thoughts and emotions. He is so good. He says "My sheep hear My voice" (John 10:27) and His voice is not in the wind or the earthquake, but comes in a still, small voice (1 Kings 19:11–13). There will be little pictures or thoughts that come to our minds in soaking; those are ways He talks to us. If any negative thoughts try to come in, keep pushing them out and relaxing. Take no thought of anything except meditating on your verses and the face of Jesus. This is an example of Biblical meditation and it takes practice: a mind that is full, not empty.

It's our privilege as a child of God to be able to enter in and receive His lavish love. And we will eventually be able to soak in Him without music because we will know how to center ourselves in His love. And all the while, He is creating a precious and beautiful garden in our hearts that reflects our intimacy with Him. He loves our intimacy and the Holy Spirit is the one that can bring us to the Father and break the orphan spirit that separated us and restore us back to our relationship. The Holy Spirit causes us to cry out for our Abba Father. Our Papa God. Eventually, you will be able to feel so comfortable in His kindness that you are able to hug Father God, sit on His lap, have Him show you things, look into His eyes, or ask Him why He loves you.

If we are having trouble connecting with His love, we can also try forgiving our own dad and mom and releasing any hurts from our parents to the Lord. And our spirits will start to rise up over our minds and its busyness and we'll let His love rush into our souls. We have been given a heart of love and He is an ocean of love inside us. And we get to the point where we burn inside to love Him even more every day. Not only that, He pursues us *relentlessly* every day.

> And I ask him that with both feet planted firmly on love, you'll be able to take in with all followers of Jesus the extravagant dimensions of Christ's love. Reach out and experience the breadth! Test its length! Plumb the depths! Rise to the heights! Live full lives, full in the fullness of God.
> —Ephesians 3:17b–19 (MSG)

Step 9

Every day I have learned I need to choose to practice resting in my Father's great big love. It is abiding, sitting, dwelling, and letting Him overflow. It is by far the most rewarding and deeply healing experience I have ever found. This step is critical for anyone who lives a life filled with stress. Soaking in quiet worship music and meditating on Scripture will eventually train you to become relaxed and connect to the Father so you can receive miracles anytime and anywhere. We simply must learn to rest and God always blesses our rest. I heard a Catholic saint once say she loved to be alone with God in the secret place because that is where she soaked up all the sunshine of His love. Wow God! Receive this prayer:

Prayer to soak in and encounter the Father's lavish love: Father, I want to have such an intimate relationship with you that I would be healed of the orphan spirit and cry out "Abba Father!" I don't only want knowledge of you, I want to *experience* you. Help me to rest and to lay aside every worry and circumstance and open my heart up to you and your love. I come to encounter you right now, so I soak in soft, anointed worship music, and allow myself to be still and quiet. I lay everything down at your feet and enter your throne of grace and mercy. I embrace you Father, I come as a child who enters right in. Father, make me to lie down in green pastures and lead me to the quiet brook of bliss. I soak in your delightful, crystal-clear river and let you restore my soul. I enjoy you, Father. I thank you that you return me to innocence as I am washed in your lovingkindness. Anoint me with the fragrance of your Holy Spirit and give me all I can drink of you until my heart overflows. Father, I breathe in your healing love over and over again. I ask that you reveal to me how much you love me. I thank you for creating me and making a beautiful garden in my heart. Your infinite love for me will never fail. I keep resting, soaking, and receiving all that you have given me here today. Thank you for your gracious healing. I want more of you! In the name of Jesus, amen.

Chapter 10

Believing for the Miraculous

Now faith is the substance of things hoped for,
the evidence of things not seen.
—Hebrews 11:1

GOD CAN DO millions of miracles in a moment and still never lose any power. The earth weighs 5.972 sextillion metric *tons* and God is upholding it and all things with the Word of His power (Hebrews 1:3). He spoke and trillions of stars were created. Miracles are easy for Jesus. He is a God without limits. He is Omnipotent, which means He is able to do *anything* and is unlimited in power. *And* He gives His Spirit to us without measure and even says. . . whoever believes in me *will* also *do* the works that *I do*; and *greater works than these will* he do. . . (John 14:12). Hallelujah! When you ask God for one of His promises, He wants to provide it. Why? Because He loves you and has a victorious plan for you and has made a commitment to us as our faithful Father. We have a covenant with Him and He can be trusted to uphold His promises of love. He delights in our well-being. Our job is to ask and then to believe we receive with faith like a child and keep pressing in for it until we have it.

How do we receive a miracle from God? By joyous expectation and faith in His amazing grace, by framing it up and speaking it out, by thanking Him for it, and by participating in the miracle and trying it out by faith. Another way is to go over all the miracles of Jesus in the gospels. Study them and learn from them. Build faith by watching and reading about the miracle testimonies of others on YouTube and on the internet. You are building hope and desire that God wants to do one for you too. You must also see the end result. If you can see it (imagine it), you can have it. They told me to imagine I was eating all different kinds of foods and wearing new clothes, and then to thank God for it.

I have seen God do so many miracles for others, I have lost count. If you believe miracles can happen, they will. The thing about miracles is that we can't figure them out. So don't bother. The minute you start to reason about things, you end up in doubt. Just believe and celebrate His answer! Be free and simple like a child. It says we will not enter the Kingdom unless we become as a child (Matthew 18:1–5). Children are humble and believe what their Dad says to them. They know their Dad will provide for them, in fact, they will keep asking their Dad until they get what they want. This is definitely true with our Father in Heaven.

As long as we can find in the Bible a promise from Him about something that we want, we can ask for it and believe we will receive it. So we open our hearts and expect God by grace through faith to help us. It says that if we set our love upon Him, He will deliver us. It also says if we call upon Him, He will answer us (Psalm 91:14–15). So cry out to Jesus, dream big, and believe Him!

> *Never doubt* God's mighty power to work in you and accomplish all this. He will achieve infinitely more than your greatest request, your most unbelievable dream, and exceed your wildest imagination! He will outdo them all, for his miraculous power constantly energizes you.
> —Ephesians 3:20 (TPT)

Part of my breakthrough came a little ways into my healing, from going to a ministry school where I could quickly get the Word of God deep into my being. People were telling me about a school and God told me to go to it only one week before it started. So I went to an information night for Destiny International School of Ministry at Jake's House Church. The Presence of God was so sweet that night at church, all I could think about was how I wanted to be near such amazing love. I walked out of the sanctuary heartbroken and crying because we had no money for the school and I didn't see how I could do it physically. I could drive my car there, but I still could not sit down for long periods of time or my legs would swell up.

One of the pastors caught me outside the door and asked what I thought about it. Through my tears, I said I loved how it sounded, but I had physical challenges and no money. He told me they had one fellow last year who had physical problems too and that God's grace got this man through. Then, he told me, "You know, if it's God's will, He will foot the bill. So, just come." I went home amazed by the faith of this pastor who had so much love in his heart! How could this man believe like this? My head was spinning. Could my dream really come true?

I discussed it with my husband and he agreed I could go, but he was really unhappy about the financial obligation considering our tremendous mountain of debt. A few days later, a previous neighbor came over and I told her the story about the ministry school and how it would be fantastic to go to something like this. She was a Christian and she thought I should go for it too. I prayed for God's will on it. It had to be God's will because I did not want to cause any more financial trouble for us, as my health problems had already put a huge strain on our budget and on our relationship. Our bank accounts were empty and our credit cards were charged to the maximum, mostly because of all the medical treatments and expenses for me. Those feelings of "it's all my fault" came at me with full force. It was a huge guilt trip.

So I cried out to God, over and over, to hear His voice. Finally, I shouted out, "Command me, God! Command me and I will do it!" I felt He wanted me to do it, but I needed a strong word, so I fasted and prayed that night too. Then God spoke. He gave me a dream about a prayer I had been declaring out loud from a bookmark card. At the top, it said, "This is my commitment of love and loyalty between me and my Lord. I will be His chosen one that contains no contamination or compromise." And it went on to quote other Scriptures, including 1 Samuel 2:35, "Then I'll establish for myself a true priest. He'll do what I want him to do, be what I want him to be. I'll make his position secure and he'll do his work freely in the service of my anointed one." That dream burned in my heart and cleared up any doubt in my mind. This was God prophetically declaring my destiny. It was a commitment between us of love. My world turned upside down that day.

The next day I turned in my application and I met with the pastors for an interview. They encouraged me to come, but they felt like God was saying I was a full-time student, not a part-time one. A full-time student? God was truly pushing me out of the nest. It was thrilling and so very scary, but it was what I secretly wanted too! That day they prayed and declared over my mind complete wholeness and proper memory function, and also for provision for the tuition. So I went home, and the minute I walked in the door my neighbor called, to my surprise, and said she wanted to give me a scholarship for two-thirds of the cost of the schooling. Wow! I was totally blown away and my heart soared with joy and thankfulness. How good can God be? So I really knew for a fact that I had a call from God. It had been a wild nine months, with so much healing and so many miracles. But there was more to come.

When I started school I had to stand and sit and stand again. And Jesus would not let me feel sorry for myself. He was doing it with me and giving me the courage I needed to up my game. I had to figure out how to eat a sack lunch with very limited food choices. I realized I was still really limited in diet, clothing, mental ability, and stamina. But God! I kept telling Him that He sent me here. So I would say out loud, "I *can* do all things through Christ who strengthens me" (Philippians 4:13).

I was really pushing my faith, way out on the limb. But Jesus would tell me "Just believe." And the miracles kept happening through being obedient. I couldn't pray while I was concentrating on lectures, so I just had to trust Him by faith. It was like the ten lepers; it happened "as they went" (Luke 17:11–19). The second week I could sit longer with no trouble. Eventually, sitting did not affect me anymore at all. Impossible? That's what I thought. But God asked me to be faithful with the little and He did the impossible.

We are called to live long and healthy lives. We are not meant to be sick in any way—spirit, soul, or body—and we do not have to accept it. And with God as our supernatural Father, He will help us receive that health and He will even give us the faith and the grace to do it. God is not mad at us; He is radically in love with us. When we invite Him into our hearts, He will change it all. The healing that I received was a process. However, the very best healing to receive from God is immediate and instantaneous. He is totally and awesomely miraculous. *Today* is the day of salvation. His freedom is now! He wants us well today, not tomorrow.

> But let him ask in faith, with no doubting, for he who doubts is like a wave of the sea driven and tossed by the wind. For let not that man suppose that he will receive anything from the Lord; *he is* a double-minded man, unstable in all his ways.
>
> —James 1:6–8

To receive your miracle, you can't be double-minded. You have to believe you have received it through the cross. You need to have *one* thought and only *one* thought, and that is you are already healed. Like the woman with the issue of blood, she said to herself over and over, "if I just touch the hem of His garment, I shall be made well." Her only thought was that she was about to receive it. There was no doubt! (See Mark 5:25–34.) God showed me several times that I couldn't be thinking anything else but that it was finished!

One time my foot was bleeding and He said: "No, I want you to walk by faith, not by sight; ride your elliptical machine anyway and take no thought about it." And the bleeding stopped. The sense realm is where the lying symptoms are birthed. You must rise up above it in the Spirit.

Another time, my shoulder was out and through prayer I was not getting breakthrough. So He told me: "Set your face like a flint, ignore it, and lift weights." Believe me, my flesh thought I was crazy, but it got healed. So stay in the Spirit and follow Him closely and do what He says.

There are many ways that God can heal us. But the main thing is that we come to Him. Ask Him for your miracle! And start declaring out loud that you are healed. Then surrender yourself into His hands and rest in His peace as you keep your mind set on heaven. He can do it! Don't *limit* the way in which your miracle can come to you. We are coming to a limitless God. He is looking throughout the earth for those whose hearts are loyal to Him, to show Himself strong for them (2 Chronicles 16:9). And there is *nothing* impossible to those who believe.

Jesus is said to be the express image of the Father's person, who in the Old Testament named Himself as the Lord Who Heals You, Jehovah Rapha (Exodus 15:26). All through the Old Testament, Father God healed the people who served Him. He kept them as His people. Now we have a new and better covenant in the New Testament. We see that Jesus went around doing good and healing *all* who were oppressed of the devil (Acts 10:38). It also says that when they put people at His feet that He healed *every* kind of sickness and disease (Matthew 9:35). And there is a case where a leprous man said to Jesus, "if it is your will, you can heal me." And Jesus said, "It is my will, and I will heal you." And He did (Matthew 8:1–3). So it is God's *will* to heal us and restore us and He wants us well.

The Father proved Himself as a Healer when He put His only Son on the cross to die for everyone's salvation and healing. It is called the atonement. He was the atonement for our sins and for our healing. *It is finished.* Which means we already have it, past, present, and future because Jesus conquered it all on the cross. In fact, we have been translated out of the enemy's kingdom into the Kingdom of the Son of His love. God canceled the accusations written against us, having nailed it to the cross and triumphed valiantly over the enemy of our soul. Jesus has totally and absolutely defeated the devil forever! (Colossians 2:11–15.) We have been set free from oppression, we have been set free from the enemy's kingdom, and we have been set free from sin. We have actually died to it, and now live for righteousness. Jesus has paid for everything, including our healing. Everything now is about the blessings of the cross. We are about receiving His blessings.

The gospel is to spark our desire to be healed by Jesus' work at the cross. Just as children are simple and believe in God, we are to believe for our healing with all our hearts like children. Our desires are important to God. With God, the cross is always now. If you are saved now, you are healed now. Be open and be playful and let God be in control. The Holy Spirit's job is to help us receive it. Your heart is the place where you believe it and receive it; don't doubt it. If your spirit and soul agree, then your body will follow along like a little puppy.

Also, if we believe we have been healed, we will test it out after we get prayer. We take the risk and try to do something we haven't been able to do before (James 2:14–22). Be looking for the miracle and what God is doing. And thank Him for it. As many times as we do this, we can receive our miracle by faith. Remember, every day is a new day with God. So every time we come to Him for healing, it's new. Doubt cannot stop us, Jesus runs right over it. Keep asking. Jesus also healed them "as they went," which means we need to participate in our healing with Him. A lot of times the miracle happens when we test it out, not when we pray. Stretch out boldly for your healing.

If you are having trouble, ask Him to heal the deep places of your heart all the way to the DNA level. Find out where the blockage is, or ask Him what lie you are believing and you can then repent of it. Then ask Him to tell you the truth to replace that lie. This truth is now your new declaration to overcome the lie, so continue to declare the truth out loud and keep those lies and familiar spirits out. Remember there is no shame or condemnation if you didn't receive your healing, just keep going and be relentless. Also, there is no set formula with Jesus. Some people respond better to different methods. Just do whatever works best for you and Him. The point is to get healed. He needs to give it to you, so be listening.

In the appendix, I have included some promises on faith that will help us believe God. As we confess them out loud, it activates our faith. We don't beg God when we pray. We pray from a position of victory. We take the promise we need, confess and declare it done and thank God for it. Our words are containers! Give God something to work with by speaking it out. Imagine it, see it, and believe it with passion. And thank God for it ahead of time by faith.

Step 10

God wants us to believe in miracles and He wants to do one for you! In fact, He is eager. Jesus is the *yes, yes, yes*. Miracles are easy for Jesus and the Holy Spirit can teach us how to receive and believe for them like a child full of faith. There are instant miracles and there are also progressive healings; the point is to get your healing either way. So believing with childlike faith, we create atmospheres rich in miracles by praising, by believing what Jesus did on the cross, by speaking it out, and by trying to walk that out by faith. Keep your eyes on Jesus the author and finisher of your faith.

Prayer for miracle healing: Father, I receive a new measure of childlike faith and expectation to rise up in me to believe you for the impossible. Love and compassion are flowing out of my heart and I simply relax and come to receive from you. I believe in miracles! I draw a line in the sand and do not allow thoughts of doubt or unbelief to come against me. I command every demonic and foul oppressive spirit to leave my body now, and go to the feet of Jesus. I release the healing power of the Holy Spirit to fill my body from head to toe, cleansing, healing, refreshing, restoring, renewing, and making new my every cell. I declare that I now live in the blessing of your divine health in my spirit, soul, and body. I declare that I am a believer and I am healed and whole right now. Thank you for healing me. In the name of Jesus, amen.

Chapter 11

Creating an Extraordinary Marriage

*Marriage is the beautiful design of the
Almighty, a great and sacred mystery—
meant to be a vivid example of Christ and
his church. So every married man should
be gracious to his wife just as he is
gracious to himself. And every wife should
be tenderly devoted to her husband.
—Ephesians 5:32–33 (TPT)*

ONE LOOK INTO his eyes and I was caught up.
I saw a sparkle, a glimmer of a knowing. Was this
love at first sight? I was curious, thrilled, and excited as we danced and occasionally locked onto
each other's eyes. In 1980, on my 21st birthday
at a disco dance club, my future husband turned
to the first person behind him and tapped me on
the shoulder. He said, "Would you like to dance?"
I said yes, I would. And we danced, and danced

some more. Then we fell in love and one year later we were married and we were off to create the life of our dreams.

My husband was a wonderful man from the start. We journeyed together through the ups and downs as innocent beginners in this thing called life. We had no idea how good nor how hard it could be. We started off really well, and then things began to fall apart with my illness. Finding no answers, the only thing I could do was to keep researching on my own, and keep up an optimistic attitude with my husband and children. But our best plans did not materialize for our family and it was heartbreaking to see our dreams get crushed. My husband and I tried to stay communicating, but neither of us understood what was going on with my health. And we started to avoid talking about the negative, hiding it deep inside. As discouragement and depression set in, our ability to stay in a healthy and vibrant relationship slowly deteriorated. My husband and I each built up walls around our hearts protecting the inner child inside of us who needed great quantities of love to survive the trauma of what was happening.

Since everything in the universe is connected, just one person who is sick will affect the whole.

And so it is in the body of Christ. For though we are many, we've all been mingled into one body in Christ. This means that we are all vitally joined to one another, with each contributing to the others.

—Romans 12:5 (TPT)

My being sick affected our whole family, and particularly my marriage. It was rough, really rough, on our marriage. I remember praying, "help me, God, that my husband can make it through this." Faced with severe allergies and the resulting eczema, dermatitis, and burning skin, it was painful to be touched and this caused a lot of strain on both of us, especially my husband. But there were times of little breakthroughs and highlights of joy in our family, and I would enjoy their stories of school and work and what was happening in the world. However, even though my husband and I had the best of intentions, there were hidden judgments, fear, guilt, and shame in both of us. Not being saved yet, we didn't know where to turn. We made the best of each day as we could, talking and living life like roommates, trapped in illness for years. Waiting. Waiting for help to come from somewhere. Continuing research, and more research, and going nowhere. And finally, letting go of it, just to survive.

But Jesus! When we got saved, Jesus had a different idea and it was a Spirit-filled marriage. I literally got challenged almost every day by following Him. He had radically great ideas and wanted me to do them right away. He encouraged me to be loving and to keep loving. "This is a love walk," He would say. I had to keep up with Him and keep those negative thoughts out.

No one has ever gazed upon the fullness of God's splendor. But if we love one another, God makes his permanent home in us, and we make our permanent home in him, and his love is brought to its full expression in us.

—1 John 4:12 (TPT)

Jesus was making His permanent home in me and showing me how to love too. He was very confident He could teach me how to do this! And He made it so fun, He literally blew my mind with His joyful attitude! He taught me the joy of loving and appreciating what was good. One day I went around the house where I was alone and homebound saying, "I love my house, I love myself, I love my floor, I love my husband, I love my family, I love my view, . . .I love my furniture." And gratitude broke out in my heart and I went to bed that night, literally vibrating with love and joy. It was such a lesson for me, to talk about what I loved. It was so simple yet so powerful. It wasn't that I didn't love, but I wasn't saying it. And the more I said it, the more I felt it. And *love* changed my atmosphere into joy. He taught me to sing through my day, and to let go of being stuck. He would say: "Just play, just sing, just worship, or just dance. Get out of your head, that's how breakthrough works."

At the Healing Rooms, they kept praying as part of the healing, that the Lord would heal my marriage. I never asked for that because with my limited sight all I could see was that I was very sick and had so many physical problems. But it was Jesus' heart and now He was my King and He was praying it out through His prayer team. And I continued to get prophetic words over my marriage. God has a gift of incredible love for his married couples, and He knew what I needed. He delights in and celebrates the best in His beloved, like in the Song of Songs 1:15, He says: "How beautiful you are, my darling! Oh, how beautiful! Your eyes are doves" (NIV). And I would cry and thank Jesus, because I found out that God's idea of marriage was like an incredible dance of romance, harmony, and oneness. It is a beautiful blessing of deep and flowing intimacy and God wanted me to have it. And He wants you to have it too.

Sometimes you come in for healing in your body, but Jesus knows what will heal your heart. He heals from the inside out and gives us beauty for ashes (Isaiah 61:3). Because the child in both of our hearts was broken, we needed to face those issues with the help of the Holy Spirit. So we worked on all those feelings that had been buried: rejection, disappointment, hopelessness, distress, fear, offense, nervousness, perfectionism, helplessness, and victim mentality. My husband and I took a few marriage classes and learned that we were both avoiders. We avoided all those awful feelings and everything else and stuffed it down inside. But God calls us to:

Rather, let our lives lovingly express truth [in all things, speaking truly, dealing truly,

127

living truly]. Enfolded in love, let us grow up in every way *and* in all things into Him Who is the Head, [even] Christ (the Messiah, the Anointed One).
—Ephesians 4:15 (AMP)

How Jesus explains it is that we must face each other and be honest, listening to and honoring the other when we have a problem, telling him or her the truth with lovingkindness. One person shares and the other listens and shows it by repeating it back. He also wants us to know men and women are different, each having different needs. And all of us also have a love language that thrills our hearts and make us feel really loved by the other. So we both started to look at these truths and started to tiptoe back into communicating again.

Jesus goes for deep relationship, so deep that He would die to have us back. He is not a surface God. He knows us completely and so He wants us to share that joy with our spouses as well. So for me, I had to take the risk and start sharing feelings that normally I avoided, and walk on the water with Jesus, believing He could teach me how to communicate all over again. No surface conversation, but getting it all out on the table with honor. And keeping nothing hidden. For example, if I was upset about something, Jesus had us sit down, and I would tell my husband the feelings I felt. And we would reconcile it with forgiveness. So we courageously admit the problems and feelings that keep coming up, being honest with each other, and tenderly loving each other, and God takes that confession, forgives us, and cleanses us from it.

> If we confess our sins, He is faithful and just to forgive us *our* sins and to cleanse us from all unrighteousness.
> —1 John 1:9

A real breakthrough happened for us relationally and physically when we found an amazing book called *Love after Marriage*, by Barry and Lori Byrne. And we followed their protocol for inviting the blessing of the Holy Spirit into our marriage and asking Him what His goals were for the marriage. Honoring the Holy Spirit's presence in our marriage has been the most profound healing of all. The Holy Spirit's whole way of being is full of wonderful counsel and gracious unity. His promise of blessing loving harmony in a marriage is as follows:

> How truly wonderful and delightful to see brothers and sisters living together in sweet unity! . . .This heavenly harmony can be compared to the dew dripping down from the skies upon Mount Hermon, refreshing the mountain slopes of Israel. For from this realm of sweet harmony God will release his eternal blessing, the promise of life forever!
> —Psalm 133:1, 3 (TPT)

With the Holy Spirit's amazing help, my husband and I have fallen in love all over again. Are we perfect? No. But we are on our way. We started doing prayer walks together and setting aside time every week for a date night. We make a commitment to pursue each other. Every now and then we treat each other with back rubs, dancing, playing games, and giving encouraging words and blessings. Most importantly, we have started blessing each other's spirit to be above the soul, and to be the one in control. We are learning to live from the heart, not the head.

In the midst of healing both of our hearts and marriage, the Holy Spirit was able to miraculously heal my body of PMS and an ovarian cyst. And it's all connected. Our bodies suffer from all the emotional and relationship problems. So don't assume like I did, that your marriage is not connected to physical problems. We both have been profoundly healed and brought back into unity through learning how the Holy Spirit cares for us as a married couple.

God blesses His married couples with rich and overflowing love, sweet harmony, and wonderful intimate relations. And your marriage deserves to be healed and reconciled. Join in the wonder of surrendering it all to the Holy Spirit. He is a genius at healing. Commit to making up with your spouse today. The Jesus kind of love is radical because He cherishes and esteems the other higher than Himself. There is no selfishness in the Kingdom of God. It's all about serving the other, honoring the other, helping the other succeed, and blessing the other. Imagine being cherished by your spouse the way Jesus cherishes you. He forgot totally about Himself and threw Himself entirely at the cross because you were the joy set before Him. This is the great mystery. This is how Jesus loves. If you imitate God and do that, why wouldn't your spouse become extraordinary, talented, and famous? If you both do it, you have the potential to take the whole world for Jesus. Come on! I am working on it. Let's all work on loving our spouses like Jesus. We can do it through Christ!

The enemy, on the other hand, has a huge hatred of our marriages. Mine was almost destroyed, but God has healed us in every way. My husband and I have renewed our love and our vows and we are best friends now. My heart is for you to take this testimony as your own. God can heal your marriage once you invite Him into it. There is nothing impossible for Him. Once you and your spouse get into unity and agreement with each other and the Holy Spirit, there is no power on earth that can stop you.

Step 11

We are all connected and if one member of the family is sick, chances are there needs to be a family healing or marriage healing as well. When I got saved, God's plan was to go after my whole family, and love all of us back to health. His love is full of nonstop miracles! So my husband and I learned to communicate the deeper issues we wanted to avoid, and to pursue and bless each other every day. Turning our relationship over to the Holy Spirit was the goal. Then we were able to get into loving harmony and unity. And loving, honoring, and cherishing each other has been deeply healing and rewarding for us both. So my prayer for you is that you begin to minister to your husband or wife as you learn about the precious and unique person God made him or her to be.

Prayer for a powerful and Spirit-filled marriage: Father, we thank you for the love and affection of the Holy Spirit and we surrender our marriage to His guidance and counsel. We declare together that we are committed to our covenant of marriage and will press in to reconcile and heal it in every dimension, not only for ourselves but for our family. We ask you, Holy Spirit, to set the goals for our marriage and to help us follow your plan. Keep our hearts open to love and affection, forgiveness, honor, fun, and communication that keeps nothing hidden. We declare our marriage is extraordinary and we are going the extra mile to keep it that way! In the name of Jesus, amen.

Chapter 12

Warriors Never Give Up

Through faith's power they conquered
kingdoms and established true justice.
Their faith fastened onto their promises
and pulled them into reality! It was faith
that shut the mouth of lions.
—Hebrews 11:33 (TPT)

THE BIBLE SAYS not to back down! We must seize not only our personal destinies but our family legacy as well. In addition, we are to raise up the sons and daughters of God. God's men and women were mighty and took the lands back from giants. In Judges 6 and 7, God sent an angel and told Gideon—who thought he was the least of his family—that "The Lord is with you, mighty warrior." And even though Gideon was full of excuses that he was weak, God put him up alone against the whole region to save Israel. God would tell Gideon, "Go in the strength you have and save Israel. Am I not sending you?" And this word from God so blew Gideon's mind that he actually asked

God to prove by test that it was Him speaking. It was God, all right. And God was calling Gideon to go out by faith against tens of thousands with just a small army. God called him out! And he is calling you out too. He is saying *you* are a mighty warrior and He is fighting beside you. The Lord is with you!

No matter what situation we are in, God calls us to think like we are champions! There is nothing too hard for our God. He can literally conquer every giant. There is a story about when God's children were crossing over the Jordan and going in to possess their inheritance. There were giants in the land. Caleb fought alongside his brothers and sisters and beat down the giants to help them get every bit of their lands, houses, and bounty. Now it was Caleb's turn and at 85 years of age he said: "Give me this mountain!"

> Now therefore, give me this mountain of which the LORD spoke in that day; for you heard in that day how the Anakim *were* there, and *that* the cities *were* great *and* fortified. It may be that the LORD *will be* with me, and I shall be able to drive them out as the LORD said.
>
> —Joshua 14:12

Caleb drove out those giants with the Lord. It didn't matter his age, or what the situation looked like, it mattered that the Lord was with him and had made him a mighty warrior. Just like in the Bible, we are also taking down the giants, and it means we can't think like a grasshopper. We have an omnipotent God inside of us who loves this thing called life and He is a genius at it. He told me: "Face those giants of fear, sickness, and doubt. Be strong and courageous. Get them off your mountain. I AM in you." So I wanted my mountain. When are we going to get sick and tired of it all and rise up and say: "God, give me *my* mountain! I want *my* mountain! I take *my* life back."

I have had this hand-written note on my bathroom wall since the first few years of my healing: *your attitude will determine your altitude.* And it would encourage me to see myself like God saw me and not to give up. You have to realize it's not all God—you get to choose. That's why He calls you a champion. You choose life, you choose with Him how far you want to go. *You* choose! You do the natural, and God will do the supernatural. Joel Osteen would say, "You make a move and God will make a move." We all have the same promises from God. But it's your *willingness* to go for it that will determine your victory!

As my first year of healing went on, I continued to get small breakthroughs in food. "I kept thinking, how am I going to overcome this, God?" Caught in the grip of fear, it was scary to try a food and then wait one to three days to see what would happen. It was such a mind game, especially after only being able to eat two foods for three years. Years of failure was all I knew.

But the real amazing miracles happened when I went on weekend or week-long outreaches. I asked my pastor, "How I can go on these things with so many limitations?" And he said, "You'll have to do it by *faith.*" So I did, and I ended up sleeping places that stretched my capacity to the max. I stayed in the homes of people who had pets, sleeping on the floor, in a sleeping bag, and eating all kinds of foods because that was all that was provided. I was also expected to get near paint, cleaning chemicals, and vacuuming fumes as part of our outreach servanthood. Having been diagnosed with multiple chemical sensitivities, these were things that would have devastated me and left me incapacitated for months. I had to lift my hands, knowing I could not do this without God. Did I have multiple chemical sensitivities? Not with Jesus in me! He would not let me be defeated. I could do all of it as I trusted God. Let me tell you, I would come home rejoicing because I had stepped out in faith, and then I refused to go back to the old routine. Now I had my breakthrough, and no one could take it from me.

One time, on an outreach in Sacramento, CA, I had a bad cold and was really sick with a sore throat and sinus infection and on and on. I couldn't even sleep at night because of severe headaches. I had even called my husband to get me a plane ticket home, but he said, "No, you can do it, you'll be all right." I felt backed into a corner. I was around lots people serving God in public so I could not fight off the cold by declaring the Word of God out loud. I could only pray in my head and keep my thoughts straight. It was a real fight. But Jesus can't be backed into a corner. He always gives us a way out.

All they were serving to eat was pasta and pizza and foods like that. Wheat was the only food left that I had not gotten back on. Now why would God bring me here if I couldn't eat the food? So my friend told me a story about her pastor in Israel. A woman came forward for prayer that had food allergies. And she kept coming regularly for it, never getting the breakthrough. So the pastor finally said very roughly, "Look, Jesus already finished it; when are you going to take it?" It was God saying: "Hello. . . are you listening? I am right here." And that word shocked me so much, that I took my food allergy healing too, meaning that I just started eating the pasta and pizza and sandwiches. Oh, it was so good to eat everything I wanted!! I wouldn't take no for an answer. I pushed in harder. And the cold got even worse, and my nighttimes were full of painful headaches and the fear of food reactions. But I was so confused and scared about what was causing what, I couldn't tell if it was an allergic reaction or the cold virus. And since I couldn't go home, I kept on eating. I refused to be that sick person. I fastened my faith onto what I wanted, and I pulled it in. And I got my healing and have been eating wheat ever since!

I had read so many lies about trying this diet and that diet to heal the body, I had literally wiped out all my foods and almost died from the lack of nutrients. But when I stepped out in faith on the water with Jesus, without looking down, I got it. I got the victory and all my foods back, and you can do it too. Just take this testimony. *Just take it!* God was able to take the harm meant by the enemy, the cold and being stuck in California, and turn it into a fantastic victory! Not only that, He was able to turn me into a real warrior in the midst of it. You have to realize what *you* are made of now. And it's God inside of *you* and He is indomitable. And that means He is too strong to be defeated or discouraged.

We are called to never give up because we can do all things through Christ who strengthens us (Philippians 4:13). Never, never give up on your promise from God. I had an experience one time where I was caught in the battle of the mind and I was hearing lies, and my mind was spinning trying to fight, but then I saw the face of an angel. Over and over, I cried out for God to help me and it seemed like I wasn't getting anywhere. Where was He? I knew He was near but I could not feel or hear Him at all. I was getting into desperation after an hour of this torment. I said, "No, I don't believe this lie, I believe God said I am healed. No, I don't feel this feeling; I feel good." And over and over I fought by confessing and holding onto the truth of the Bible. It was a real shouting match. But I was being worn down.

Finally, I saw a face above me. It came through clearly, and it was so beautiful in kindness, gentleness, light, and glory that it totally captured my mind and heart. All I could see was this beautiful face beckoning to me, and my eyes were drawn strongly to it. It was an angel that was communicating to me through its eyes and strengthening me. . . "Look up, look up at heaven," the angel said, "Set your mind on heaven, and heaven's glory will overcome you and break through." And I felt a surge of relief that God had sent me help and I wasn't alone. I cried with gratitude and the angel broke off the mental torture. It took a while, but I didn't give up, and God finally got through to me by sending an angel.

Jesus told me later what I needed most of all in that moment was the weapon of worship, to sing to Him with all my heart, to put my hands up and not wrestle. Because it would have lifted me out of my thinking patterns. You can ask God what would be your most effective weapon in different situations. And you can keep increasing the weapons you have on your tool belt, i.e., worship, prayer, fasting, Bible study, communion, confessing, meditating with the Lord, praying in the Spirit, thanksgiving, etc. You are not limited to one. But don't get drawn into praying from the place of a victim. You pray from a place of victory, success, and faith. You can also shout from that place of victory as well and it's powerful. Pray short prayers, believe, and then praise God for the answer. Sing to Him and worship. Singing can help you over. This is one of your best weapons. Worship God and look up, look up at heaven, expecting Him to answer. You have covenant rights to have your prayer answered—so let your faith and hope soar—keep asking, seeking, and knocking and the door will be opened.

With my health, I could never give up. I immediately got better with prayer. But there was a real fight for my life. I had to hang on like a pit bull to God's promise of healing. There was no way I would let go. If I let go an inch, the enemy took a mile. In the beginning, it was like two steps forward, one step back. I would have a few victories, then a defeat. But I kept charging forward. Going week after week for prayer. Insisting to God, to myself, and to the world, God said He can do it and He is not a man that He could lie! I have seen many people receive their miracle and then have it get stolen from them by the enemy because they did not know how to contend with the promise of God. But by the fierceness within me, I was going to possess that promise, and that included keeping everything else out of my mind and having my focus on heaven. We have to be aggressive in our stance. They call it "taking it by force." We take our promise by force and those mountains have to move out of our way. It's your promise, so don't back off. It's not a weak or timid process. God told me, "Nancy, you cannot be passive!"

> And from the days of John the Baptist until now the kingdom of heaven suffers violence, and the violent take it by force.
> —Matthew 11:12

This is the place where we have to lose all that pride and consider maybe we are worth it, maybe

God loves us more than we can possibly imagine, and maybe we can dare to hope again! When we, in humility, tell the prayer team our issues, and they pray the prayer of faith, God will raise us up (James 5:13–18). And while we are waiting in faith on God for the healing and it seems like nothing is happening yet, keep thanking and praising Him and creating miracle atmospheres by singing, decreeing, and prophesying about your healing.

If it seems that you are not able to receive your healing, you may need to look more deeply at the root cause of it. I got my healing "as I went" partly because my faith kept building, and I was seeing it happen before my eyes and I was saying: "Oh my gosh, if Jesus can do that, why can't He do this?" So I dealt with things one at a time, kind of like peeling an onion. We have to be willing to change our habits and the way we think.

There are things that may be stumbling blocks to a healing and if you don't seem to be improving, don't give up! At the present time there are some deeper healing ministries out there that work with the Holy Spirit like Sozo, Liebusters, Elijah House International, or Theophostic Ministries. You can look online for one near you. I have tried Sozo ministry and even got the training because I received some great freedom. Especially in the area of learning to ask the Father questions and listening to Him speak truthful answers. He is the truth and the truth is freeing indeed.

Remember during the waiting, that God can work all things for your good. There is tension and mystery sometimes between the prayer and the answer. I got my healing over time so I would tell myself "No problem then, I can let go and relax a little because even though it's hard, He can work it *all* for my good." And then there is another promise too; He always leads us in triumph. *Always* (2 Corinthians 2:14). And again, He knows the plans He has for us, plans for good and not for evil (Jeremiah 29:11–13). So therefore:

> My brethren, count it all joy when you fall into various trials. Knowing that the testing of your faith produces patience, but let patience have its perfect work, that you may be perfect and complete, lacking nothing.
>
> —James 1:2–4

Communion

Communion is one of the most powerful secret weapons against the relentless attacks of the enemy. I saw an article written by Kenneth Copeland that suggested taking communion three times a day for revelation of your healing and as a technique for warfare. So I tried it. I would say a prayer first, blessing it and then would read communion Scriptures over it. I did this every day for a year. I was determined to receive my healing and would not give up. Sometimes I would feel better from it, or God would encounter me and sometimes I would see Jesus. But I was taking it by faith and expecting to get healed by

His stripes. In the Old Testament in Exodus 12:1–28 they ate the Passover lamb and put blood on the doorposts and over 2 million people walked out healed with not one feeble person among their tribes (Psalm 105:37). This slain lamb was a type and shadow of Jesus. They also ate manna from heaven in the desert and their clothes never wore out nor did their feet swell (Deuteronomy 8:4).

Wow! That is incredible and I would meditate on that miracle. And I would pray to Jesus that He would do that for me too. I wanted my miracle provided in the Passover lamb. In John 6:35 (TPT) it says "I am the Bread of Life. Come every day to me and you will never be hungry. Believe in me and you will never be thirsty." And in 1 Corinthians 11:24–25 it says: "Do this in remembrance of Me. Take, eat; this is my body broken for you. In the same manner *He* also *took* the cup after supper, saying, 'This cup is the new covenant in My blood. This do, as often as you drink *it,* in remembrance of Me.'"

So every day that year I came to Jesus and communed with Him by faith for His promise. And we came to be really close friends. And as I took communion, I thanked Him for what He did for me and gratitude would fill my heart. It became a healing meal for me with the Lord. There is healing when our sins are forgiven and there is also healing in His stripes. Also be sure to examine your heart to see if there is anyone you need to forgive. In order to take it rightly we must have the revelation in mind that His body is *life* and *life* more abundantly and His blood forgives our sins forever. He offers us a healing opportunity every time we take it.

I would refuse to sit at the table of demons (which includes sickness). . . and I would proclaim "This is the cup of blessing and I am sitting at the Lord's table. I draw a line in the sand with sickness or strongholds and refuse to have them, and I decree Isaiah 53:5, which says, "He was pierced for my transgressions, He was crushed for my iniquity, the punishment that brought me peace was on Him and by His wounds I am healed."

Always remember: the enemy has been defeated. It is finished! Believe that. We get up now and fight the good fight of the faith, and enter into God's blessing of rest by believing we have it and taking no thought about negativity. It's really important to remember our battle is one of faith. We rest in the promise seated in heavenly places in the place of victory. We do not strive, we surrender our cares by putting ourselves on the altar and releasing our worries to Jesus. It's the attitude that God is going to do this, so I am going to dance out my worship, or sing, or do whatever He is leading me to. And it is also one of walking by faith, not by sight or by sensations. God does the healing and the miracles, and our job is to believe and to receive. Then we cast out any thoughts that come against His promise, and keep speaking the promise over ourselves. So hang on and see God do glorious miracles!

Step 12

Step 12, then, is: once you get that miracle, you need to keep it. So hang onto your promises! God calls us to be more than conquerors (Romans 8:37) who have already overcome the world. I thought I could back off a little once I got healed. But I still need to stay in the presence of Jesus, keep my mind renewed, stay in the Bible, hold fast to His promises, and worship, because the enemy walks around like a roaring lion (1 Peter 5:8). But that's okay, I can also sing, dance, and shout the high praises of the Lord all day in the joy of the Lord! Basically, by the prayer of faith, we should not have to put up with anything! So we must set our faces like a flint and take by force what we know is ours and never give up and never quit asking. Keep your hopes and expectations high because love never fails. And remember, it's settled, it's finished, and it's done on the cross.

Prayer for relentless pursuit of His Promises: Father, thank you I am a mighty warrior, and warriors don't back down or bow to the enemy. Father, give me the strength to go in and take possession of the land and my promises and even to take them by force. My work is to enter the blessing of your rest at the throne, knowing my healing is finished. I steadfastly continue to believe and cast down every vain imagination that comes against me. Father, I take the healing meal of communion, rightly believing for my healing. And Father, you said you do not fail to perform your promises and I believe it. I am already healed by the stripes of Jesus, therefore I take authority and speak and command that healing to manifest by faith now in my spirit, soul, and body. In the name of Jesus, amen.

Epilogue

Jesus, how do I finish the story, when it's all a day-by-day continuing journey? I am constantly learning new things about God, myself, and others, and it is a never-ending process. But I would like to say that, thanks to Jesus, I have been able to return to a regular life again. I can't thank my husband enough for his steadfast loyalty and prayers. My marriage is totally blessed, and God has helped us to pay off all our debt and to buy a home again. I have two amazing sons that are both married and now I have my first grandson, and another on the way. It is it such a dream come true! I never thought I would live to see grandchildren. Thank you, God, for miracles!

Just like all of us, I still have to continue to take good care of my health. There have been times even very recently where I still battle off colds and pain. Sometimes the enemy just plain tricks me into believing a lying symptom. And it's hard! Believe me, I know how hard it is for those in a really low and painful place. But I know Jesus is there fighting and I am getting smarter at this thing called faith. I will continue to stand on the incredible blessings of His promises and love.

I have continued to volunteer at the Skagit Valley Healing Rooms for the last four years because I absolutely adore seeing people receive their healings. I have gone through the three-year program at Destiny International School of Ministry with Pastor Jeshu Ram and was invited on staff for two years. I have been blessed there with so many encouraging prophetic words that my heart still soars with the Lord's courage. When I was down, they lifted me up. And whenever I was sick, they all surrounded me with compassionate hands of prayer. Then my Pastor, Keith Kippen at Jake's House Church in Arlington, Washington, licensed me as an outreach pastor for his church.

They found out that I couldn't help telling everyone about my Jesus at the grocery stores, libraries, parks, and praying for people and handing out food on the streets. God would put them on my heart and I have seen Jesus do some crazy healings, salvations, and amazing prophetic words out there. My prayer is to see America saved and all my brothers and sisters come home. My pastor, an artist friend, and I have put together some beautiful Scripture cards that are now going out to over 50 prisons through a ministry at our church. I have traveled to Mexico, Israel, and most recently Cambodia, where I spoke at a women's conference.

My prayer for you is that you come to be friends with this most amazing Jesus, that you go into the promised land, and that you take hold of your inheritance. I am cheering for you and you can do it! Go for it and receive your miracle! God wants you to walk in total health and wholeness and into your fantastic destiny. God had a dream about you and He wrapped you around it. It says in Jeremiah 1:5, He knew you before He formed you in your mother's womb. He even wrote about you in a book. And as His masterpiece, He is working within you daily to create His exquisite poetry for all of us to read.

Join me as I go with Jesus into a new adventure every day and worship Him with all my heart. We dance, sing, play, and learn to love to the best of our abilities. My life verse has never been more true today than it was the day the Lord gave it to me: ". . .the *joy of the Lord is your strength*" (Nehemiah 8:10).

Appendix

Decrees

These decrees have been put together by paraphrasing Scriptures so that they can be declared over yourself. God has exciting promises for us to be able to speak and create our world. Make them with faith and volume, believing that you receive. You are sowing seed in order to reap a harvest because God's Word will not return void (Isaiah 55:11). He does not fail to perform His Word. Remember, speaking these out loud will build your faith because faith comes by hearing, and hearing by the Word of God (Romans 10:17). You want your mind to come into agreement, but it is really all about heart faith. We are called to believe with our heart and then make the confession with our mouth. We also want to have our spiritual eyes opened to see ourselves as Jesus does. Let Him sanctify the eyes of your imagination and you will be blessed as He shows you great visions. Use that visualization He is giving you as you pray and speak it out (Jeremiah 1:12). And the deeper you get into the glory light of heaven, the quicker things will manifest. Thank you, Jesus!

Who You Are In Christ

I am a child of the Most High God, I have been baptized into Christ and have put Him on, and I am an heir according to the promise.

—Galatians 3:26–29

I am a sacred temple of the Spirit of Holiness. I don't belong to myself, for the gift of God, the Holy Spirit, now lives inside my sanctuary.

—1 Corinthians 6:19

I am God's chosen treasure, a priest who is a king, a spiritual nation, set apart as God's devoted one. I am called out of darkness to experience his marvelous light. He claims me as His very own so that I will broadcast His glorious wonders *throughout the world.*

—1 Peter 2:9

I have been redeemed from the curse of the law, I have received the promise of the Spirit, and all the blessings of Abraham have come upon me.

—Galatians 3:13

I have been raised up with Christ the exalted One, and I ascended with Him into the glorious perfection and authority of the

152

heavenly realm, and I am now co-seated as one with Christ!

—Ephesians 2:6 (TPT)

I love God with all of my heart, and I love my neighbor as myself.

—Mark 12:30–31

I am a new creation, the old has gone, and I have now been given a ministry of reconciliation.

—2 Corinthians 5:17–18

I am kept as the apple of God's eye, and He hides me under the shadow of His wings.

—Psalm 17:8

I go into all the world and preach the gospel. I am a believer that drives out demons in the name of Jesus, speaks in tongues, has supernatural protection, and lays hands on the sick and sees them recover, the Lord working with me.

—Mark 16:15–20

I have stopped imitating the ideals and opinions of my culture, and am inwardly transformed by the Holy Spirit through a total reformation of how I think. This empowers me to discern God's will as I live a beautiful life, satisfying and perfect in his eyes.

—Romans 12:2 (TPT)

I trample on scorpions and snakes and over all the power of the enemy.

—Luke 10:19

I am consistently growing in all the fruit of the Spirit: love, joy, peace, patience, kindness, goodness, faithfulness, gentleness, and self-control.

—Galatians 5:22-23

Faith Scriptures

I live in the faith that is active and brought to perfection by love.

—Galatians 5:6 (TPT)

I am crucified with Christ and the life which I now live in the flesh, I live by the faith of the Son of God, who loved me, and gave Himself for me.

—Galatians 2:20

I have the faith of God within me.

—Mark 11:22

If I can believe, Jesus tells me, all things are possible to me.

—Mark 9:23

I speak to mountains to be removed, and do not doubt in my heart, and whatever I ask for in prayer, I believe that I have received it, and it will be mine. And if I need to forgive anyone, I do it.

—Mark 11:23–24

I believe my faith is now and that it is the substance of things hoped for the evidence of things not seen.

—Hebrews 11:1

I ask, believing and not doubting, because the one who doubts is like a wave of the sea, blown about and tossed by the wind.

—James 1:6

I abide in Him, and His words abide in me, and I ask what I desire and it shall be done for me, By this My Father is glorified, that I bear much fruit; so I will be His disciple.

—John 15:7–8

I walk by faith, not by sight.

—2 Corinthians 5:7

I believe Jesus is able to do what I ask, and according to my faith it is done.

—Matthew 9:28–29

I exercise my faith, otherwise it is impossible to please God; He is supernatural and He rewards those who earnestly seek him.

—Hebrews 11:6

I have confidence in God because I know that if I ask anything according to His will,

He hears me. And if I know that He hears me, whatever I ask, I know that I have the petitions that I have asked of Him.

—1 John 5:14–15

Healing Scriptures

Father, Your Word saves my soul and has become a part of me. It flows in my bloodstream. I give attention to Your words because they are life and medicine to me. You sent Your Word and You healed me.

—James 1:21; Psalm 107:20;
Proverbs 4:20–22

I speak blessing to every cell in my body: you are normal in Jesus' name. My cells do not succumb to any disease. Jesus took infirmities and He bore sicknesses. Therefore I refuse to allow sickness to dominate my body.

—Matthew 8:17; John 6:63

I feel good and I feel great! The great I AM lives in me and He took every sickness away and has already healed me by His stripes.

—Galatians 2:20; 1 Peter 2:24

I bless the Lord because He has forgiven all my iniquities, healed all my diseases, and redeemed my life from destruction. He satisfies my mouth with good things so that my youth is renewed like the eagle's.

—Psalm 103:2–5

I submit to You, Father, and resist the enemy in every form that he comes against me. He must flee from me. I resist him and I enforce Your Word. I am blessed with a strong and healthy body.

—James 4:7

My words are wise and bring healing, so I speak the Word of faith to my body. I command every internal organ to be perfect now. Body, I declare that you are healed and made whole, inside and out.

—Proverbs 12:18

God's love is like a fountain of living waters all around me springing up into everlasting life. He loves me with the same passion that He loves Jesus.

—John 4:14; John 17:23 (TPT)

I am an overcomer by the blood of the Lamb and the word of my testimony. Jesus gives me life and life more abundantly until it overflows.

—Revelation 12:11; John 10:10

The same Spirit that raised Christ Jesus from the dead dwells in me and He thrills my body with new life. I am enfolded into Christ and I am an entirely new creation.

The old order has vanished. Everything is fresh and new.
—Romans 8:11; 2 Corinthians 5:17 (TPT)

Father, I will not listen to any lies that come against me. I will be faithful to Your Word. With shouts of grateful praise, I will lift my hands to You, for my salvation comes from You alone.
—Jonah 2:8–9

Father, I love Your joy, it is my strength and my medicine. I drink in the fullness of Your joy daily and You heal my spirit, soul, and body.
—Proverbs 17:22; Nehemiah 8:10

God protects me! He commands His angels concerning me to guard me in all my ways, so no harm will overtake me, and no disaster will come near me.
—Psalm 91:10–11

References and Suggested Resources

Bevere, John. *The Bait of Satan Workbook* (Messenger International, 2008)

Blake, Curry. *Divine Healing Technician Training* (John G. Lake Ministries, 1997)

Byrne, Barry and Lori. *Love After Marriage* (Regal, 2012)

Capps, Charles. *God's Creative Power for Healing* (Capps Publishing, 1991)

Capps, Charles. *The Tongue, a Creative Force* (Capps Publishing, 1976)

Chapman, Gary. *The Five Love Languages* (Northfield Publishing, 2015)

Gossett, Don and Kenyon, E.W. *The Power of Your Words* (Whitaker House, 1981)

Hagin, Kenneth. *Healing Scriptures* (Faith Library Publications, 1993)

Hagin, Kenneth. *The Believer's Authority* (Faith Library Publications, 2005)

Hamon, Dr. Bill. *Speaking in Tongues CD set* (Destiny Image, 2012)

Hunter, Joan. *Power to Heal* (Whitaker House, 2009)

Meyer, Joyce. *Knowing God Intimately* (Faith-Words, 2015)

Mills, Joshua. *31 Days to a Miracle Mindset* (New Wine International Inc., 2010)

Nelson, Miranda. *Take Your Place in the Kingdom* (Living At His Feet Publications, 2014)

Osborn, T. L. *Healing the Sick* (Harrison House Inc., 1986)

Silk, Danny. *Keep Your Love On* (Red Arrow Media, 2013)

Wommack, Andrew. *You've Already Got It* (Harrison House Publishers, 2006)

Made in the USA
Middletown, DE
11 June 2019